My American Odyssey:
An Ordinary Man Called Upon by His Country to do An Extraordinary Thing.

Written by Donald Byers
Edited by James Byers

Byers Publishing, Inc.
189 East Third Street,
Wyoming, PA 18644
jim@337thinfantry.com
570.328.2941

My American Odyssey:
An Ordinary Man Called Upon by His Country
to do An Extraordinary Thing.

Written by Donald Byers
Edited by James Byers

First Edition, 2017

ISBN-13:978-1544805009/ISBN 10:1544805004

Dedicated to all soldiers
who have risked and sacrificed their lives
for freedom and family.

My American Odyssey:
An Ordinary Man Called Upon by His Country to do An Extraordinary Thing.

Written by Donald Byers
Edited by James Byers

Contents

Foreword

"I felt scared when we first started, but I was okay after a hundred yards."

That phrase really hit me. I read it over and over again to try to comprehend the anxiety and dread my grandfather felt as he crept along that Italian highway. After several reads, I felt his fearful anticipation of an enemy ambush or a hidden landmine. That phrase hypnotized me, putting me in some sort of state in which I saw the war through my grandfather's eyes. For a moment, it was me who was creeping along that highway. I scanned the treelines and looked over my shoulders for Germans. I heard gravel crunch under my boots and my own nervous breathes.

Thud. I blinked and saw that his notebook had slipped out of my hands onto the floor. My heart quivered from the thought of my grandfather in fear for his life. What if he had come under fire? What if he had been killed?

It was then that I realized that there was more to his story - and I have been searching ever since.

Historians and veterans have written thousands of books about World War II. But **My American Odyssey** *differs from most books because the story is told from the point of view of an average soldier. The author included personal experiences and details about the war that can't be found in some books. Readers will notice that, as the war progressed, his attitude fluctuated: between a humorous, good-hearted patriot to a depressed, angry G.I..*

My American Odyssey *is based on a short story Donald Byers wrote about his state-side basic training several years after his discharge from the United States Army. Those handwritten and typed accounts make up the early chapters while the latter portion of the book is derived from notes he scribbled into pocket-sized pads while in combat. Letters that he wrote to family and friends filled in pieces of missing time and reveal his personable side.*

A lot of research was necessary in order to learn more about the influences and experiences that shaped his perceptions of the people and places that he encountered. Most of the work entailed inquiries to government agencies, trips to his hometown, and conversations with surviving friends and family. Afterward, it was clear to me that Don Byers was just an ordinary man who was called upon by his country to do an extraordinary thing.

Although Don's later life didn't involve military warfare, he did fight personal battles that tested his fortitude. Back injuries he suffered during combat made daily life uncomfortable and sometimes unmanageable. Medical records stated that fatigue and body aches made it difficult for him do an honest day's work. He endured the pain instead of accepting defeat and worked as much as his body would allow - something he learned while in the Army.

His most dire period came months after the birth of his first child, a daughter named Ann. She was diagnosed with spina bifida and later died following an operation to treat the debilitating disease. Don witnessed death before in Italy, but this was not something that he could march away from.

By 1958, Don had made the goals that he set for himself while a soldier a reality. He was married and was given another chance at parenthood with the birth of a second daughter, Janet. He was working and very involved with his church's choirs and Boy Scout troop despite the back aches.

But nothing could have prepared him for the loss he was about to incur. Unbeknownst to him, his body was invaded by the polio virus which attacked his nervous system, killing him at age 44. He died before he could finish telling his story.

This book not only details a soldier's sobering accounts of a war, it also tells of the personal battles that he endured while attempting to live the American Dream. A dream that lured his grandparents from England to the United States. A dream that he fought so hard to defend.

While researching and writing this book, I was able to learn things about my grandfather and love him even though I had never met him. My mission was to help him finish his story, for his sake and for mine. I wanted this book to be a memento for my family and maybe inspire some readers to sit down with a veteran in their family to learn more about them.

And when it comes to WWII veterans, the time to sit down and reminisce is now.

Jim Byers, *Editor*

Chapter 1:
Leading to War

1941

The news reports were menacing. German Chancellor Adolf Hitler and his Nazi regime sought to impose their radical ideologies upon the people of Europe. By 1941, the political party had risen to power cloaked by promises of tranquil prosperity and was enacting its plan to conquer the continent by brute force.

Germany invaded neighboring nations Poland and France and was well on its way to controlling the remainder of Europe. The continent was divided into allies, neutralists, and the enemy. Hitler formed alliances with Italy's leader Bennito Mussolini and Japan's Emperor Hirohito to create the Axis, which collectively plotted world domination. Germany had made a non-aggression pact with Russian leader Joseph Stalin.

Britain was the biggest challenge for Hitler. The country was considered a super power because of its legendary navy and colonies around the world. The English Channel posed an obstacle for the Germans to cross, so their air force mercilessly bombed the British Isle. The Brits fought to protect their shores while they battled the Axis in Africa for control of the Mediterranean Sea.

The Nazis seemed invincible. Most countries couldn't withstand Germany's blitzkrieg attacks, bullish Panzer tanks, or Luftwaffe air-strikes. Each victory bolstered Hitler's ego and he eventually decided to defy the pact with Russia in June. The ambitious war plan named Operation Barbarossa sent German forces across the Russian border marching towards Leningrad. Stalin vowed to crush Hitler and joined the Allied Forces led by England.

Amidst all of this, the United States remained neutral. President Franklin Roosevelt pledged his support to the Allies and sent supplies to countries that fought against the Axis. The President slowly, and secretly, organized the American military to prepare itself in the event that it would become involved in the war.

October

Donald Byers read the disturbing newspaper headlines from the comfort of his home not thinking that these events might ultimately affect his life. He lived in Pennsylvania, thousands of miles away from the turmoil brewing in Europe, so there was little reason for him to be concerned.

The twenty-six-year-old worked as a clerk at a corner grocery store a couple doors down from his family's home on Wakeling Street in Frankford, a quiet blue-collar neighborhood northeast of Philadelphia. He was the son of full-blooded Englishmen and devout Methodists who worked as masons, but manual labor was not attractive to him. He aspired to do something more with his life. College was an option, but he really wanted to concentrate on his music. Don had played the violin since childhood and sang as part of the choral groups in high school and church. His baritone voice could also be heard at the weddings of friends and family.

The majority of his spare time was spent with his girlfriend, Ann. Their paths crossed not far from his home near Frankford Hospital where she worked as a nurse. They had been dating for several months, going to movies, dinners, and parties. During the summer, they spent hours on the beach during his family's annual vacation to Wildwood, New Jersey.

In the summer, Don received notices for physical exams and in October the Selective Service ordered him to report to the local recruitment office. He believed that the chances that he would be called upon to serve his country were slim. Days after his twenty-seventh birthday, he had a physical examination: he was in average physical shape, 5'7", and 148 pounds, and his hearing and vision were standard. The Army chose to classify him as 1B, on reserve, most likely due to his age.

Despite the examination, Don doubted the possibility that he would enter the war that was now engulfing most of the world. He downplayed those chances with Ann, who feared that the United States might be the next country to become involved in the conflict.

A month later, on December 7, Japanese pilots attacked the American naval port at Pearl Harbor in Hawaii, destroying ships and killing more than a thousand sailors. This heinous attack forced Roosevelt to declare war on Japan, which prompted the Germans to declare war on the United States.

Pearl Harbor was a call to action for many Americans and Don was no different. He went to the recruitment office to enlist in the Army, but his 1B classification disqualified him from volunteering. And Ann also heeded the call. She worked as a nurse at Frankford Hospital and planned to use her nursing skills to care for wounded patriots.

The Army soon changed its mind about Don Byers. He received another notice from the Selective Service in February to report for an examination on March 9. Days after the exam, he got a letter from the Selective Service that informed him that his status had changed from 1B to 1A: he was being drafted into the military. Don was instructed to report for duty on May 15.

The time for Don to enter the war drew closer and he could no longer doubt that fact. He knew that he could survive the outdoors, thanks to his days as a Boy Scout, but the only gun he had ever fired was for games on the boardwalk. His biggest concern was how this might worry his mother who was very protective of her only son.

Don also wondered how this might affect his relationship with Ann - would their love be able to withstand the separation? He had no idea where he was headed or how long he would be gone. Would she be patient enough to wait for his return? If he were disfigured in some way, would she still love him?

And, like many solders, he faced the possibility that he might not return.

I have set nothing down in notes on my time in the Army until we entered the "combat ~~stage~~". So, for the period preceding that, I must revert of the "Official Division History" and my own recollections.

It would be very tedious for both you - (as the reader) and I - (as the recorder) - ~~for me~~ if I were to set down the names of all the men and officers I've come in contact with from time to time. Some few will be mentioned in passing, those who are not named are probably better forgotten!

Don Byers

Chapter 2:
Reporting for Duty

1942

May

When I found that my draft board had reclassified me from 1B to 1A, I decided that it would be a good idea to loaf before my entry into the Army. It puzzled me to learn that I was fit to be drafted into the same Army that wouldn't accept me when I tried to enlist. Later on, I would be puzzled about the Army twenty-four hours a day.

On the morning of May 15, my father and my friend, Charles Dixon, accompanied me to Draft Board 23 not far from my home in Frankford. Did the Army think of the psychological effect of having the draft board in a police station? After the usual flag-waving orating, another draftee and I were put in charge of a large group en route to the U.S. Army Recruiting and Induction Station for the final physical exam.

For the first of many, many times I viewed the tricks Mother Nature had played on us when she handed out the various representative parts of the male anatomy. Up until then, I had been rather modest about my nakedness, but the Army soon took care of that.

We lined up in single file and the parade was on. The doctors grunted and mumbled as they pushed us hither and thither. We were so confused that we didn't know just what they wanted to look at next. And when they mumbled instructions to do several things one right after another, the result was more hilarious than the Marx Brothers at their zaniest. After being slapped, pinched, stabbed, and probed, they finally tagged us and shook their heads sorrowfully.

Throughout the day, someone would holler "All those who haven't eaten, outside!" So several of us, when we had nothing else to do, would fall in line every time. I think we had three lunches and three suppers.

At 4:30 p.m., they separated the black and white men before they swore us in without mental reservation and sent us on our way to the train at the B&O Station. On the way to the station, some guys' suitcases flew open, spilling underwear, bottles of liquor, and etcetera on the pavement. One poor fellow had to pick his things up three or four times, until he finally growled "Ah, the hell with it!" And there it may still be lying.

After separating those going on the train from those who were just there to say good bye, we finally shoved off for Fort Meade, Maryland. There were naturally a few drunks whooping it up, so we didn't get a chance to feel blue. Frankly, I was still confused from that merry-go-round at the armory.

Buses met us in Baltimore, and so, then to camp. The first thing we did was line up along the wall, with our pants down at our ankles. How easily I blushed in those tender days. After a quick bite of cold spaghetti and an introduction to the G.I. coffee (battery acid) we trotted off to bed at last. The barracks had at least three times the number of men that it was built to hold, but who cared. I was so tired I thought I could sleep immediately, but I hadn't reckoned with the night sounds of the men.

Somehow, Morpheus and I got together.

The next day, the rat race started - and how those privates made us step! They ran us here and there, then back again all day in the rain until the sergeants began to go crazy - I mean even more so. We saw movies, attended lectures, took mental tests, had interviews, and then were issued uniforms. Since much has been said, written, and drawn about the fit of Army clothes I need not add my ravings. I'll merely pause to nod in the affirmative.

It amused me to watch an officer approach a group of new men. Some men would take off their hats, some would salute, and others just rolled their eyes and gulped.

Before each meal, we lined up in three ranks in front of our barracks. We noticed that for breakfast the first rank led off to the mess hall, then, at noon, the second rank led. And at night, the third rank led us off. So several of us began to fall in the particular rank that led at first. It worked the whole time we were at that camp.

I must set down at this point our experiences with the various needles with which we were tortured. A private led us to a long low building and when we were herded inside, someone hollered "Strip!" So we did. The medics were lined up on either side of a narrow passageway. As men passed, various parts of their bodies were daubed with alcohol. I stopped at one point and a G.I. jabbed me with a knitting needle, but after the first twinge it didn't bother me. The next stop was between two sadists who very quickly gave me the works. I took two steps and thought someone had hit me in the back with a sledgehammer. When I got out into the air I felt much better. From a vantage point, I waited for the color to come back into my face and watched them carry out five or six big men, six-footers all.

We boarded a train for destination unknown number one. I was certain that I was a cinch for quartermaster because the interviewer was so enthusiastic about my civilian experience. Oh, how disillusioned I would soon be.

The pullman cars were rather crowded, but we were so excited that we didn't mind it. For after all, how were we to know that overcrowding was standard procedure in the Army. Every time the train jerked we all hollered "Jesus Christ!" There was no liquor aboard this time and I had no smokes. It was a lot of fun despite the guard duty and no chances to wash. We learned that we were headed for Camp Shelby, Mississippi, by looking at the tags on a sergeant's duffel bag. For some unknown reason, we went through eight states to get there. From Baltimore, we went through Pennsylvania, Ohio, Illinois, Indiana, Kentucky, Tennessee, and then to Mississippi.

On arrival, we were jammed onto a truck and whisked away to a large tent theater. We were sorted out according to our new companies, and our little group from Frankford began to disintegrate. Some of them I would never see again - they are still in Italy.

When we settled in tents in our company area, I asked a sergeant on the cadre, "What quartermaster outfit is this?" His face lit up with a diabolical smile as he replied, "This is the infantry." There and then I knew that my country had betrayed me.

The next day, our training exercises took us off the easy road marked "Civilians Only" and down a narrow, winding, rocky road that finally led back to the civilian road. Some of the best men who started out couldn't keep up with us.

Our company commander, Captain V.P. Yletchko, was a West Pointer. He was a soldier from head to toe, and it didn't take an act of Congress to make him a gentleman, either. Right from the start we knew he was the boss. Each morning he'd stop in the messhall and as soon as he reached company area he'd proceed to bawl out the mess sergeant. As a result, we had the best chow in the Regiment.

The days following were all cut from the same pattern: calisthenics, close-orde drills, shots, clean tents, clean rifles, clean this and that and so on, far into the night. Everything was by the numbers, in other words, all together and at the same time. We had lectures and movies by the dozens on military courtesy, sex, discipline, insurance, and everything pertaining to the Army. The Company Commander stressed close-order drills more than anything else. As a result, at the 4th of July parade we were the best drilled outfit in the Division. We even got a commendation from the Assistant Secretary of War who was in the reviewing stand at the time.

In July, we went out to the rifle range for the next phase of our training. Our first experience was sleeping in pup tents on the ground. Boy, was that rough. We hiked ten miles to the range and were all tired on arrival, but we worked far into the night setting up the camp. Since I was picked for the wire section, in my spare time I put out the phones necessary to run the range, helped lay the wire, and at night I was graciously permitted to operate the switchboard. They were so nice to me.

I had never fired anything bigger than a 22 rifle on the boardwalk at Wildwood, so I looked forward to firing my M1 rifle as a dubious pleasure. Several men were knocked flat from the recoil and others got black eyes from not ducking the bolt fast enough. I was ready to apply for a bow and arrow — and I was sure I could convince them. However, after the first few shots I began to enjoy firing the cannon. My final score was enough to permit me to wear the marksmanship badge, but rarely did I wear it for I have a horror of badges and buttons. Someone might mistake me for a Boy Scout or something.

Upon returning to camp, we found ourselves in another area, a real barracks now. And a new company commander, too. Capt. "Mad Russian" Yletchko went to a hospital for an operation. Sure hated to see him go, though. He was tough and strict, but his first thought was the health and comfort of his men. Once, when he thought we weren't getting the proper food, he hollered all the way up to the Commanding General of the Division. We got the food and he got ten days restriction from the Regiment Commanding Officer.

By now we were really beginning to work on our specialties. Some of the guys were wiremen and some in the intelligence platoon. Our training started to take shape now. I was attending a communication school, run by the Division Signal Corps, for instructions on wire and switchboards ever since the beginning of July.

Our new company commanding officer became Lieutenant Smith and Lieutenant Hubert Speck, "The Speckled Bird," was our commanding officer and right from the start they confused us beyond measure.

Byers earned the rank of Private First Class on August 14, and was assigned a Technician 5th Grade to the Headquarters Company of the 337th Infantry Regiment, 85th Infantry Division, of the 5th Army.

We took our first long hike sometime in August: twelve miles. The poor timing and general conditions caused more than 500 men to fall out before we finished.

In the fall, our field training began. The officers got lost more often than we did. Need I say more? Gradually, the training lengthened from one day to two weeks, and by October we were more proficient in our appointed jobs.

The weekends were wonderful because we were allowed to get passes, but in order to get one the barracks had to be spotless. Ditto clothes and rifles. Then, we had to stand in the bus line from one to three hours in order to get to

Byers stands inside a hutment (a wooden tent) at Camp Shelby in September.

Hattiesburg (a whistle-stop that looked like a honky tonk sideshow) then onto another train to New Orleans. Pete Mason, a fellow wiremen, and I met a very friendly family who we visited occasionally, which made the weekends much nicer. We heard a lot about southern hospitality, but never saw any until we went to New Orleans.

Most of the rebels were loud mouthed, narrow minded, egotistical morons. Everything they had was better than anything anywhere else, yet most of them had never been more than a hundred miles from home. The Texans were the worst.

The day before Christmas, we were thrilled by the thoughts of a twenty-five mile forced march. Well, we made it in seven-and-a-half hours and I couldn't make up my mind which foot to limp on at the end. And no one in the Company fell out. The Regiment Band, which had been with our Company, was transferred to Division so there no noise to blast me out of bed in the morning.

On New Year's Eve, the entertainment was a fight in which Bill Knott gave John David a lovely pair of black eyes - such pretty colors.

Chapter 3:
A Soldier in Training

1943

A letter Byers wrote to his uncle, Harry Bailey:

January 31

Dear Harry & Kate & Nancy:

Just a few hasty lines to say thanks for the cookies. The boys think they're the best they ever ate. We're on the run all the time. Problems two-three-four days at a crack, but they're a lot of fun. No sleep or food, but we eat enough in between problems to make up for it. We may go on maneuvers soon, but don't tell Mother for awhile. We may go in April. I get my sleep whenever I can. I don't get it on the problems so I have to grab it when I can. We're having lots of fun, though. No matter how tough things get, something always happens that gives us a laugh. Someone always falls in the mud or something like that. The days get pretty dreary sometimes, but the sun finally comes through. And that's the way life goes, too. Well, it's time to get some shut-eye. I have to get up at 3:30 a.m., sooo - to bed, to bed.

Love to all of you -
Don

In February, we went on a three-week maneuver period just outside of camp. By now, Lt. Sprague was our commanding officer and Speck our company officer. Sprague was definitely bucking for captain, so he worked the hell out of us. He never gave a thought to the feeding or comfort of the men. It was bitterly cold and quite a bit of rain. We thought it was very rugged.

Later that month, we swapped Major General Wade Haislip for Major General John Coulter. We thought the first one was a whip. Well, it wasn't long before the CD on the shoulder patch stood for "Coutler's Dogs."

By this time, "Smilin' Jack" was our commanding officer, with Lt. Dick Sweeney as executive. "Big Picture" Sweeney was a regular guy, really an enlisted man with bars. He gave us lots of

Out on a pass, Pete Mason and Don Byers meet a friend for a few drinks in March.

breaks, too. Coutler had a reputation for being miserable, so we were ready for him and we handed back just as much as he gave. Our new first sergeant was a Texan with an I.Q. of fifty, at the most. He was from a rifle company and tried to treat us like a bunch of dogs, but we put him on a merry-go-round that he never did get off.

In April, we went to Louisiana for big maneuvers and our enemy was the 93rd Division. A life of pup tents, dirt, swamps, snakes, man-eating insects, and lots of work. We learned to work in blackout, from the book. Later in combat, we threw away the book. We got used to missing meals, sleep, and comforts. Of course, we couldn't expect the officers to miss those things. And they didn't. The Regiment Commanding Officer had a special toilet and never had to sleep on the ground or miss a meal. His command car carried a special flag so that he could go behind enemy lines, then come back and plan counter tactics. What a way to fight a war.

Lt. Colonel Stanley Lauferski always yelled about men smoking at night in the blackout. Lauferski was nearly as wide as he was high, and his long nose was into everything. One night, he came out of his tent and saw a lot of small lights going on and off. Immediately he dispatched a second lieutenant to make the men stop smoking. After crashing around in the brush, bashing his shins on logs and bumping into trees, the second loot discovered that the offenders were fireflies.

On June 6, we left our bivouac in Texas headed for California. At the last minute we got a reprieve: Sprague was transferred out of the Division. We traveled to Merryville, LA, where we assembled before boarding the train. Our assembly area was a pasture used by the cows as well as us, and several boys managed to slip and slide. It was hot and there wasn't too much shade. We took off our equipment and lined up, and that's when the crap and card games started - big ones, too - with thirty to eighty dollars in the pot. Pete, Doc Meyers, Richard "Skipper" Gordon, and I played some friendly pinochle...that is, we tried. Between every other hand, we'd start on some detail or other, so finally we quit in disgust. After chow, they gave us our clean uniforms - what a job to stuff in our packs.

At 2100, officers started looking for men for guard duty, so I ducked and moved about three hundred yards so they wouldn't find me. Boy, there was a mad dash to get out of details. Men moved faster than they had for months.

The next day, we loaded onto a train, by the numbers, then pulled out. The berths were made up and I got a lower. I went on as a car guard at 0700. We passed Silsbee and Cleveland, Texas, before I got off guard at noon. After lunch, I played pinochle with Pete, Doc, and William Cook. Porters sure had fun calling to colored gals along the way. The conductor was from Virginia, but he knew the 30th Street Station and Frankford Junction.

The train reached Navasota where there were cotton plantations on both sides of the tracks. Then we stopped at Somerville to drill and exercise for an hour. The officers ordered us back onto the train and told us that we could get out at Temple and see the town. But when the train reached Temple, they wouldn't let us go more than fifty feet from the car. We sent a colored boy to get us some ice cream. Well, when he came back some others tried to get it off him. Boy,

what a scramble. Ice cream was twenty-five cents
a pint. One fellow gave a boy ten dollars to get
him some liquor, but the boy never came back.
The officers eventually let us cross the street
to the USO Store where I bought some candy and
cigarettes. The Catholic chaplain was really on
the ball. He came around with cards and
envelopes and collected mail. We stood around
singing before the train left. Berths were made up
at 2200 and we were in them fifteen minutes later.

On the morning of June 11, we arrived at
Sweetwater, a good size town with bungalow style
homes and a few clapboard homes. The air was
cool and clear. The porter trained us to make
and take down our berths. We traveled past oil
fields with big refineries and cemeteries set in
orchards. There were lots of potato mounds,
small bare hills, and plenty of mesquite bush-
es. I ate pancakes for breakfast as I watched the
rolling countryside. We passed an airfield filled
with avenger planes. The weather was dreary.

At Big Spring, we had a close-order drill,
then left half-an-hour later. Some guys played
cards rather than appreciate the scenery as we
traveled through the Guadalupe Mountains. There
were small ranches with little vegetation and
plenty of sagebrush. The scenery was right out
of a western movie: flat-topped hills and small
mountains; it was very picturesque. How different it was from the Pocono Mountains. When we
pulled into Big Bend, we sent some kids for ice
cream, but they resold it to someone else. What
a racket! We kept on going into the mountains
and arrived in Sierra Blanca where we played
games and did calisthenics in a natural theater
formed by mountains. The area was inhabited by
mostly Indians and Mexicans, and the town was

full of adobe houses and hotels. I watched the sunset: what a picture as it sank behind the mountains. Boy, with a foot of snow and a toboggan a fellow could have some fun.

The boys sure got a lot of liquor at the last stop. The car started to jump with the jive. There were five men in the toilet drinking whiskey without the officers seeing them. It was funny to watch them reel down the aisle as the train lurched from side to side. Every five minutes someone would stick their head into my berth and ask if I wanted a drink. Some of them couldn't find their berths and climbed into every one that was vacant until someone threw them out. We changed to Mountain Time at midnight when we passed through El Paso, but we were all in bed. I woke up in Hachita, New Mexico, at 0700. Boy, do the drunks have big heads.

That afternoon, we stopped in Tucson, Arizona, for a close-order drill. Tucson had a large Army airfield and civilian field with plenty of bombers and huge water towers. It was another modern resort town. Medics wouldn't let us buy ice cream, Cokes, or candy. They claimed we were getting diarrhea from it, but it was from the greasy silverware that was carelessly washed on the train. We left at 1700 and passed through Red Rock at 1935 and headed for Yuma. The train continued to climb higher. I watched kids ride a balky donkey as we entered Eloy at 2030. The area was inhabited by mostly Mexicans and Indians. I went onto a flatcar for guard duty at 2130.

On June 13, we passed through Ocapo and Gila. It was cold, windy, damp, and lonely on the car. I dozed in a sleep all night. In the morning, a porter on the officers' car brought me a cup of hot coffee and some cookies that the officers hadn't finished. Boy, did that hit the spot. At 0730, it was time to change shifts. I had to go through the whole train to get the relief guard. We detrained at a point about four miles east of Yuma then loaded onto trucks. Our spirits dropped to zero. All we could see was desert and mountains. There were several airbases there. Then our spirits jumped way up again when we crossed the Colorado River into California.

After a ride through the country, we turned right onto a wind swept desert plain called Camp Pilot Knob, nothing but desert. The rest of the day we worked pitching our tents and the next day we put in the switchboards. Each day we became more and more disgusted with the desert life. There was nothing but heat and sand. Our boards were set up in a tent away from the Company, and we lived in that tent. It was a quarter of a mile to chow, but we didn't mind a bit. The whole Company seemed to forget that we were around, but at calisthenics time in the morning we were sure glad they had forgotten us although we got caught once in awhile.

The training continued for weeks with the main stress on water discipline. One canteen per day for drinking and shaving, but so many fellows passed out that they had to increase the ration. The next trick was to put so much salt in the water that most of us got sick as dogs. And all that time, the officers got ice in their water and other drinks. We couldn't understand why the ice was good for them and not for us.

On July 11, I started home on a fifteen-day furlough. It was a wonderful experience riding on the crowded trains, but the seats weren't too comfortable. It was interesting to watch people acclimating themselves. Every G.I. coming into a coach looks around for the nicest girl to sit with, and the girls did the same thing. Unfortunately, I drew a staff sergeant.

In Arizona, a cute lil' blonde six-year-old and her mother, Elizabeth, got on the train. Little Janet would bring up her comic books for me to read to her. She'd curl up on my lap and we'd have a swell time. They left at Kansas City, but our friendship continued through letters.

From a station near Chicago, I sent a wire home to say that I'd arrive at the 30th Street Station, but I missed the train so I went to North Philly instead. My mom and my girlfriend were kinda burned up because they were waiting at the other station. As usual, the furlough didn't last long enough to do the things I'd planned.

Upon my arrival back to camp, I learned that a platoon had gotten lost in the desert while on a problem (*assignment*). Some of the men were still out there somewhere, so the whole Regiment was out searching for them. They had been on a night problem and an officer had given them the wrong compass azimuth. Naturally, they got lost and without water or food. By the time help got to the platoon, some had wandered off. General Coulter ordered the men to complete the problem before they had fully recovered. In *TIME* magazine, an officer stated that "the men begged to be allowed to finish the problem." (*Two soldiers were found dead and another was never found.*)

Shortly after the fiasco, we moved to another camp deeper in the desert. The nearest town was Indio, but we were fifty-some miles from there. Soon after we got settled, our real maneuvers began. It was kind of warm though — up to 160 degrees fahrenheit. Numerous flash

A letter Byers wrote to Elizabeth Lewis:

August 22

Dear Mrs. & Janet,

Hello! Well after many trials and tribulations I arrived safe and sound in the arms of my family. I missed a train at Chicago, but managed to get another an hour later. The family waited at one station, while I arrived at another one. However, we finally got together. First thing I did when I got home was to get into a tub of hot soapy water. Boy, what a feeling!

I've been going round and round ever since I got home. Everyone was so nice to me that I felt rather embarrassed at times. So many people have asked me out to dinners and parties, etcetera, that I'll weigh a ton by the time I get back to camp.

I took my gal's '42 Buick and drove to the seashore. Boy, did we have fun. Most of us in the car were G.I.s and we sure raised Cain.

We've been in another camp since July, about fifty miles northeast of Indio. They really have us where they want us this time. Nowhere to go and nothing to do. Hardly anything to eat, either. Sure helps to get a box of cookies or cake from home. Our training gets tougher all the time, but, of course, we expect it so it doesn't bother us too much. I had hoped to go to L.A. for three days, but it will have to be postponed for a while. Maybe I can look up the girl you mentioned — if I ever get there. If I don't get out of here soon, I'll go nuts! Must be the sun.

Sincerely,
Cpl. Don Byers

---

rainstorms kept things from becoming monotonous. Boy, how the rain would pour down off the bare mountains. We felt so sorry for the officers because their section always seemed to take the worse beating.

At Camp Coxcomb, we saw demonstrations of strafing and light bombing. One day, the artillery put out a barrage as a sample of things to come. That was the perfect barrage — all outgoing and none coming our way.

In the beginning of October, we were suddenly pulled off a field problem and found that we had orders to start packing. The rumors had us riding off in all directions at once. A G.I. on the inside told us our next stop was Fort Dix, N.J., before even the General found out the destination. Some of the men began to shout and sing at the news.

Before we left, I managed to get a pass to Los Angeles and Hollywood. A few of us made the trip in a station wagon and drove seventy miles-per-hour through the mountains. Boy, what a ride. I was rather disappointed in Hollywood. It was just a lot of false fronts. We spent Sunday afternoon at the Palladium. It was a fine dance-hall with bars on two levels with music furnished by Charles Spivakork. We had dinner at The Brown Derby, where we saw only one movie star, Preston Foster. All the way to California to see a Philadelphia boy.

Sunday night was rather hectic because we had to round up several of the boys for the ride back. One fellow from North Dakota persisted to help a newspaperman sell his papers, but half the time he was selling North Dakota to those passing by. He was a very happy drunk. We'd put him in the car, then we'd go off looking for another missing member and come back to find him out selling papers again.

Several days after we returned, the Company Commander, dear Capt. Seizas G. Milner — a Southerner — decided to punish us for leaving fifteen minutes early. Pete and I were punished by being restricted to the company area for a week, but there wasn't anyplace to go anyway so who cared. Shortly after this, we went back into the mountains to begin another "Battle of the Pass." We had no sooner started on the problem when orders came through to return to camp. Division passed the word down that the fighting has ceased, return to base. One of the boys misunderstood and spread word that the war was over which created quite a bit of turmoil until the rumor was straightened out.

By November, we boarded a train for the East and it was a lot of fun all the way. Lt. Col. Lauferski's Bugle Corp was on the train with us, and every time we stopped in a small town, he would assemble his boys - and puffing like a locomotive — led them and us all over town in an impromptu parade.

On this trip, we saw another part of the country, for our route took us through Albuquerque, St. Louis, Cleveland, Pittsburgh, and Philly. We made several stops in Philadelphia near Crown Can and the Frankford Junction. A couple of us had a hard time trying not to jump off.

We finally pulled into our regiment area in Fort Dix and a rush started to get the best beds in the two-story barracks. A few of us got a room to ourselves and set up house keeping to the tune of much sneering and jeering from the privates.

Just as we settled down to enjoy our

comfortable surrounding, Cpt. Milner decided that we should scrub the barracks. The outfit who preceded us in that area had scrubbed the buildings from top to bottom, but since it was against the regulations for us to rest we had to make with the soap and water. The first floor was scrubbed. Then we started on the second. Halfway through, someone discovered that the water had leaked through and soaked all the beds below. We moved everything outside and then finished the second floor. The next day, the Captain inspected the buildings, but they didn't satisfy him, so we had to do it all over again. Naturally, all this helped to further endear him to the men.

Each morning we rolled around on the ground doing toughening-up exercises then attended lecture reviews on all subjects covered so far in our training. I guess I wasn't so tough because I fractured my right elbow. The next day, we had to throw grenades and that really fixed me up. For the next few weeks, I went to the boneyard for physiotherapy treatments three times a week, but I didn't mind too much because it got me out of calisthenics and hikes.

The Commander General decided to give us a course on the rifle range, and it rained almost every day. The object being to make every man a marksman on paper; because even though a man couldn't hit the target he still passed. The weekend passes made up for the little irritations during the week. It was nice to be able to shove your legs under some home cooking.

During this time, the officers kept telling us to make out our wills and take out the full $10,000 insurance. Since the war hadn't become real to us yet, we treated it as a joke. And the inspections! Every day we'd lay every stitch out on the bed for inspection, and the officer would merely walk in one door and out the other. Soon we were ordered to clean our equipment, then pack it for overseas shipment.

In December, we boarded a train for Camp Patrick Henry at Hampton Roads and Newport News in Virginia. That move sobered us a little, although it still seemed like an adventure. We got off the train then we were ushered into barracks that had double-decker bunks instead of beds. The inspections continued, and we were issued gas masks and Allied equipment. We watched a number of combat training films that were rather gruesome but true.

For a Christmas present, the Company drew guard duty, kitchen patrol, and prisoner of war searches. I drew the P.O.W. assignment. Fifty of us were loaded onto a bus and taken to a pier at Hampton Roads to search 500 Krauts for concealed weapons. At first, we were a little nervous because we thought they were all tough and ferocious. We were surprised to find that they weren't any different than us. After we had finished, we went to a delousing station, then to a kitchen for a big turkey dinner. The boys on guard had it tough because it snowed all day.

On December 30, we packed our duffel bags and rolled our packs. The next morning found us on a train headed for the boat. And still we were wise cracking Boy Scouts. We filed up the gangplank to head for who knew where. There were no bands playing and no crowds to see us off, just a few gray-haired ladies serving black coffee to the tune of drizzling rain pattering on the tin roof of the pier.

The ship was the H.M.S. Andes, of the British Royal Mail Line, and had been launched only two years prior to the war. Before we settled down in our compartment on the F Deck, we got a tour of the ship. Our guide got lost.

We spent New Years Eve on board and pulled away from the pier at 1030 on January 1, 1944. As I stood on deck watching the United States slip away from me, old familiar faces and places went past my eyes in a kaleidoscope of memories. After I could no longer see the shoreline, I looked out across the ocean toward the imaginative question mark in front of us.

The badge of the 337th Infantry Regiment is a wolverine perched atop the latin phrase "vis et virtus" which translates to "the power of truth". The circular "CD" badge represents Custer's Division formally known as the 85th Infabtry Division which was originally formed at Camp Custer in Michigan in 1917 during World War I. The background of the 5th Army patch has a mosque to represent the native religion of the North African region where it first entered WWII. The top patch is the U.S. Army's Corporal Technician rank.

Chapter 4:
Where the Big Guns Roar

1944

Editor's Note: *There is no known journal that documents Byers'
service between January and early May of 1944. Excerpts from
337th Infantry Regiment Monthly Reports and the book The 85th
Infantry Division in World War II were used to describe some of the
combat and conditions the Regiment encountered. As part of the
Regimental Headquarters Company, he was not directly involved in
attacks on the enemy; as he focused on the transmition of information about Allied and enemy positions and reports of supplies and
ammunition. His movements followed those of attacking forces and
can be tracked by noting mentions of the* Regimental
Headquarters Company *and* wire crew.

January

Byers pondered many "imaginative question
marks" as the 85th Division sailed across the
Atlantic Ocean. How long would this war to save
humanity last? Could the Nazis be defeated?

Now, thousands of miles of ocean water
separated him from those he loved. He
reminisced about the holidays they celebrated
together and the relaxing afternoons they spent
on the beach at Wildwood. He hated not being
home to play big brother to his younger cousin
Nancy and worried about his mother worrying
about him. Adela Byers was always concerned
about her son when he was just a manager for the
high school football team, but now he was playing a more dangerous game.

His thoughts turned to Ann and how their relationship began to falter after his furlough at home that past summer. They spent the last year reassuring each other that their love would survive the war, but that became difficult after a while. The number of telephone calls and letters to each other dwindled as did the affection in their words. It was in December that she mailed him a "Dear John Letter" that expressed emotions and thoughts that she had kept secret for many months. Ann said that she noticed a change in Don and that some things about him had never changed. His idea to focus on his music rather than a career always bothered her. She pointed out how his father (who immigrated to America when he was five-years-old) never complained about working hard to provide a modest lifestyle for the family. The way that Don had become so insensitive and introverted made her feel unloved. Ann regretted writing the cliché letter, but she believed that his changes and stubbornness would always affect and ultimately end their relationship.

The length of the trip created too much free time for mulling, so Don passed the empty hours by playing cards with his comrades and sleeping (which he knew would be something in short supply in the near future).

By 1944, the power of the Axis was diminishing. The Germans were fighting a two-front war: the Russians were pushing the Nazis back into Europe and the British and Americans forced the Germans out of North Africa. Now that the Allies controlled the Mediterranean Sea, they pounced on Italy, which had withdrawn from the Axis after its army floundered in Africa and Greece. The Allies' initial invasion of Italy was led by

General Mark Clark and the 5th Army in September of 1943 - the first true land assault on the Axis homeland. At this point, it seemed the 85th Division's mission was to either support the 5th as it continued to campaign upward through Italy or battle in the Balkans.

The ocean voyage gave the soldiers a break from rigorous training, but they were still assigned tasks such as guard duty, maintenance, and radio operation. They were gathered each morning for exercise sessions then lifeboat drills. The 85th Division landed at Casablanca on January 9th. For most men, this was their first glimpse at a foreign country. The conditions were similar to the American deserts but the people and culture were vastly different. The soldiers were transported to Camp Don B. Passage where they were stationed for several days. On the 14th, they boarded cramped traincars headed for Oran. They would soon settle into Camp St. Denis du Sig, located sixty miles away to the southeast. Their quarters were located at a former P.O.W. camp surrounded by barbed wire which was soon removed since Italian and German prisoners had been relocated. The 85th's regiments practiced mountain training there for a few weeks focusing on covering fire and covert movement. By the end of January, troops moved north to Port aux Poules on the shores of the Mediterranian for amphibious training at the 5th Army Invasion Training Center.

January 30

Dear Mrs. L. -

I guess it will be sometime before I know how Janet liked her doll — I'm in N. Africa. And the mail situation is very disheartening. I have visited Casablanca and Oran. They are interesting towns, but not for a steady diet. Every Arab is filthy and ditto the towns. The best food is what we get in camp - steak today. I don't know where they get it, but the natives have plenty of money. They offer $10 for a carton of our cigarettes — but we're rationed, so we keep what we have. That sure tickled me the way Janet sat so still on my lap while I read to her. Tell her I'm looking for a letter from her.

As ever,
Don

North Africa - 1944

The 85th Division landed at Casablanca in January then moved east to train in staging areas near Oran, where they later disembarked on their mission to support the invasion of Italy which began in the fall of 1943.

February

The 85th rotated between St. Denis du Sig and nearby training camps in Azrew and Chanzy. Each camp provided different military exercises for the troops from amphibious training to mountainous combat scenarios. The amphibious training concentrated on exiting landing crafts and smaller assault vessels to prepare soldiers for landing on the Italian shores which resulted in several deaths and seriously injuries. In mid-February, Col. Oliver Hughes was assigned as the new Regimental Commander of the 337th Infantry. He relieved Col. Schweickert who had led the Regiment since their state-side service. Hughes was well versed in military strategy with a reputation for brave leadership.

February 12

Dear Harry & company -

Everything is OK, feeling fine, etcetera. While going through that snapshot holder you gave me, I found a picture of Nancy when she was three years old. It was taken at the pool with her in a new sun suit. Her tummy and her tongue are both sticking out and she has that impish look on her face. It sure made me smile. Dad and I had so much fun with her when she was little. We sure made her do tricks. Tell Kate that I sure miss her coconut pie. No one makes it as well as she does. According to the experts, the war will be over soon - maybe if those "white collar" experts had to serve some time in the infantry, they wouldn't go making rash statements. But let's hope they're right.

As ever — Don

A telegram Byers sent to his mother, Adela:

February 17

All well and safe. My thoughts are with you.

Love,
D. Byers

March

On March 8, the 339th received orders to set sail from Oran to Naples, Italy. The once pristine Italian port had been devastated by the tremendous battles that proceeded the 85th's arrival. On March 14th, they landed and were immediately split into groups: some went straight to the front line to relieve portions of the 5th Army's 88th Division. The front line was about 40 miles north near Minturno, a city that overlooked the Nazi stronghold called the Gustav Line. Those who remained spent the day and night unloading equipment and supplies until a midnight German air raid sent soldiers and civilians running for cover. The Allies had forced their way into Italy and occupied almost a quarter of the country, but the Germans were relentless in their defense. After a week in Italy, the 339th was earning its battles scars and the 337th and 338th soon anchored in the Neapolitan harbor.

The Division established a command post in an olive grove 10 miles behind the front line. During the first week of April, they conducted preparatory training for the front line with staged attacks and stream crossings. On the 8th, Field Order #1 was received from Division HQ: the 337th had to relieve portions of the 88th Division's 351st Infantry. Advance detachments, including the Regimental Headquarters Company, departed for the front line to start the relief. Troops moved by truck to the Garigliano River where some stayed to guard the bridge while others proceeded on foot to 88th positions that surrounded Minturno. There had been little activity in this area within the past two months, so both the Allies and enemy were well prepared for combat.

April 4

Dear Mrs. Lewis & Janet -

Well, I've reached another point on the G.I. circuit. Somewhere in Italy as the communiqués have it. I've seen very interesting things, geographically and otherwise.

Say, you think you have mountains in Arizona and California, but they're just hills. The scenery is very lovely, and if it weren't for the grim business over here I could enjoy it a lot more.

The news reports of conditions here are pale besides actually seeing the conditions. You folks at home should thank Him for being so far from the fighting.

As ever, Don

April 9

Dear Harry -

Somewhere in Italy...

It's a rainy Easter night, but the sun was out this morning. We had a very nice church service. I'm in good health, but always so darn hungry. Must be the climate. Never saw so many mountains in my life. However, some parts of the country remind me of western Pennsylvania, but of course not as pretty.

Tell Nancy thanks for the card and letter. I'll bet she sings like an angel. It's good training for her. She needs discipline. She'll change a lot in the next few years. I was going to send some-thing to Kate, but I never did get back to Oran again. Tell her not to despair, I'll get something yet.

My love to all, Don

Much of April was spent gathering information about enemy positions and firepower - by forces on both sides of the Gustav Line. The Allies and Axis were preparing for major offensives against each other in May; when the weather would be better suited for warfare. Some fire was exchanged, but it was more for intimidation than aggression. Groups of troops were sent out each night to patrol areas along and over the Gustuv Line. The main objective was to capture prisoners for interrogation and the secondary mission was reconnaissance. A few Nazis were captured but it was the civilians who provided good tips about enemy positions. The Division used every bit of information to decide its next course of action as well as help its allies.

The 337th's Headquarters was located in Minturno City Hall and kitchens were setup in surrounding buildings to serve companies on the line at least one hot meal a day. A shower unit was installed for the troops to bathe and they were issued new clothes and ample ammunition. The most difficult problems the 85th faced was the transportation of supplies, troops, and the dead over the traffic congested supply route from the rear areas in Mondragone to the front line. All movements were made during the night because of the enemy observation of the bridge that stretched over the Garigliano River.

As days passed, giant convoys were enroute to Italy from American and British camps still in Africa. Tanks, ammunition, vehicles — any and every thing — were on their way. Commanders on the ground and national leaders were convinced that the upcoming attack was pivatol to beating the Third Reich.

April 16

Dear Mrs. Lewis & Janet -

I'm up where the big guns roar "somewhere on the Italian front." You'll read about us, but won't know it. We've been ducking and praying. That's all anyone can do. However, I have a nice deep dugout, so I'm better off than lots of other fellows.

The Krauts are out classed, but they're too dumb to know it. Boy, I'd sure hate to have all our big guns firing at me.

We get cigs, hard candy, and mail every day. Sure keeps our morale up. If you have good hearing and a deep hole, there's a good chance you'll come out without a scratch. Some shells whistle and some sound like a train at 200 miles per hour.

Give my lil' Janet a kiss for me.

As Ever, Don

May

During the first days of May, the 337th Regiment continued to defend the assigned 4,300-yard sector called the "85th Division zone." The sector extended from the western edge of Minturno, through Tufo to the Ausente River. All three 337th battalions were on line in order, from left to right (First, Second, and Third). The front line was lightly held during daylight hours, but fully manned each night. The defense was strengthened by the installation of wire entanglements, mines, and digging additional reverse slope positions all along the line. All positions on the line were subject to hard enemy shelling and mortar fire daily. Each night, the battalions dispatched ambush, reconnaissance, and combat patrols that often made contact with

"Up Front"

Dear Harry -

*   You must have had a nice Easter. Ours was nothing compared to those other fellows you wrote about.*
*   Your letter of the 25th got here yesterday. Not bad service, eh!*
*   I get a kick out of Nancy's art work. We all got a chuckling at them. She doesn't do so bad, either.*
*   The Krauts aren't so arrogant now. American dogfaces can get just as tough as the Russians. They've proved it, only you folks back home haven't been told about it. Although people are beginning to realize that the Air Corp can't win the war.*
*   Well, it's time to get back to work again. Send some more magazines when you can.*

As Ever,
Don

the enemy. A daylight patrol by the Third Battalion captured a few prisoners.

The 337th commanders received orders to make plans to assist the Allied offensive in Italy. Initially, in division reserve, the Regiment was assigned to an assembly area in the lowland east of the bridge. Troops spent several nights digging trenches and foxholes in this area to prepare for the attack. The entire area was under enemy observation and all installations were concealed below the ground or in buildings. The cannon company moved to a northern position to support the impending attack. The 351st later relieved soldiers from the 337th who were positioned on the front line.

Regimental commanders devised numerous plans to attack and repel enemy counter-attacks. Several companies trained and prepared for offensive combat while other soldiers remained at the assembly area quiet and blanketed from enemy eyes by smoke generators. Most of the 337th moved to assembly areas near the flatlands with the Regimental Headquarters Company while the Third was attached to the 339th Regiment which marched to an assembly area in Tremensuoli.

The attack jumped off at 2300 on May 11. Troops from the 339th were covered by tremendous artillery and heavy weapons support while the 337th stayed in division reserve. Although no troops from the 337th Infantry participated in the initial attack, it was not long before its troops engaged.

Several companies from the 337th's battalions were dispatched at 0400 to assist the 339th which had run into bitter opposition as it tried to take the objectives: Hills 66 and 69. A couple companies moved out to help the 339th capture Hill 69 and the combined forces managed to get a slim hold of the Hill, but suffered heavy casualties.

The First Battalion marched out to join elements of the 339th near Tremensuoli and setup a command post. They sustained a few casualties as they closed in on the city. Upon their arrival at 0930, the Battalion was ordered to march to the left of Hill 69 to capture 66. As troops pressed onward, they came upon Capo d' Acqua, a waist-deep stream fifteen feet wide that ran behind 69. The combined forces attacked at 1400 without heavy weapons support. Big men

The Gustav Line - Spring 1944

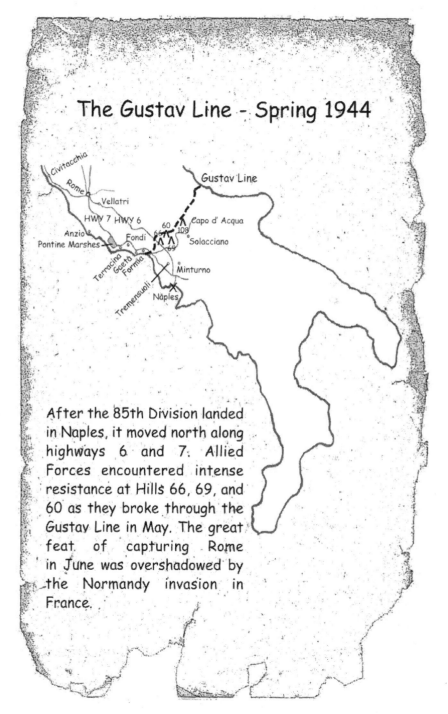

After the 85th Division landed in Naples, it moved north along highways 6 and 7. Allied Forces encountered intense resistance at Hills 66, 69, and 60 as they broke through the Gustav Line in May. The great feat of capturing Rome in June was overshadowed by the Normandy invasion in France.

* Above map based on maps printed in **The 85th Infantry Division in World War II** Schultz, Paul, L. (See **Bibliography** for more.)

were ordered to lead the attack by plunging through the stream as quickly as possible. A good strategy that put the taller men at the front (who could cross the stream easier) which in turn gave confidence to the shorter men who followed.

The troops soon took control of both 66 & 69, but were forced back by tremendous counterattacks. After more than an hour of fighting, Hill 69 was completely in Allied hands and at 1630 another attack began to regain 66. The initial rush suffered severe casualties, so the Americans fell back to 69. The desired position was heavily defended by the Germans, who hid in concrete bunkers with walls two feet thick and supported by steel beams. The small arms fire and artillery fire caused the combined forces to retreat back to Hill 69 to reorganize for another surge.

At 1830, the commanders ordered a massive artillery barrage that used dozens of 150mm and 240mm guns and that lasted more than ten minutes. Afterward, troops probed each German emplacement, killing or taking prisoners along their way. Every yard was bitterly contested by the Germans, but after much close combat and ferreting the enemy out of dugouts, Hill 66 was captured. During the operation, many casualties were caused by enemy mines, artillery, and automatic weapons. Morale was at its lowest, but following the successful engagement it rose steadily.

With Hills 66 and 69 in their hands, the troops organized a defense to prepare for a possible German counterattack at daylight. Evacuation of the wounded and dead was a serious problem as was supplying more food, water, ammunition, and replacements to the soldiers who remained in the battlefields. As the sun rose, the enemy stormed 66 sweeping every inch of the ground with machine gun fire. They crossed the crest of the hill coming within 50 yards of the Allied position. It was then that the order was given to fire and the enemy was cut to pieces by infantry and artillery fire. Every single German soldier was killed. More artillery fire was ordered to prevent the enemy from sending more troops for another attack.

Later that day, casualties were evacuated under heavy harassing fire. The enemy aimlessly dropped bombs around Tremensuoli, narrowly missing the Regimental Headquarters. Troops on Hills 66 and 69 received constant artillery fire throughout the night, but they held their position.

On the morning of the 14th, the Germans launched another attack on Hill 66 with supporting artillery fire. The fight lasted for most of the day, but again the enemy was repelled when they reached the crest. The Second Battalion was ordered to attack Hill 108 at 1500. The Battalion was supported by tank and artillery fire and achieved their objective by 1715, then reorganized their position for a counterattack. The enemy heavily shelled the hill. That evening, a company on the north slope of Hill 108 ran into an enemy force and had to pull back. They regrouped and launched a counter offensive with support from an infantry and tank company. The Hill remained under Battalion control, and eighty Germans were captured.

The next day, the Third Battalion moved forward to join the Second outside of Castellonorato. The Battalions attacked the city at 1500 with support from artillery and tanks units. The Germans viciously fought to keep their position, but the severe bombings forced them to retreat. The battalions captured Castellonorato by dusk.

On the 16th, the Germans withdrew from their positions on the line so the Second and Third battalions pushed west. Their advancements were met by enemy resistance throughout the day. At 2100, the 85th Division was ordered to halt at its present position. The break in combat allowed the troops to be issued clean uniforms and much deserved rest.

Between May 12 and 16, more than 100 soldiers were killed and 500 wounded from the 337th. The Nazis had lost their control of the Gustav Line. This defeat was part of Germany's growing problem of losing ground that they had already conquered like North Africa. Italy was now Hitler's fight and he was convinced that the Allies could be beaten back.

The 85th progressed forward taking Maranola and Trivio the following morning. The 337th's Third Battalion continued north to join the 338th and 339th regiments to bolster the attack on Formia planned for the 18th. In the morning, the combined forces entered Formia without much of a fight. At noon, the Second was sent out to pursue fleeing Germans with help from tanks, heavy artillery, and reconnaissance teams until they reached the next city, Fondi, or stiff enemy resistance.

The Regimental Headquarters collected itself to move near Formia to setup a command post. The wire crews performed very well throughout the operation, with only rare breaks in communications between the Division's command posts, despite the heavy shelling. The 337th's battalions held positions in close proximity of each other outside Formia. The 85th marched forward to seize Fondi on the morning of May 19th. The troops fought against sharp enemy fire, but by noon the city was under their control along with eighty prisoners. The First Battalion was ordered to advance with an armored unit down Highway 7 to take Terracina, but their movement was hindered by enemy fire on their right flank. The enemy's attack intensified as the Battalion approached the outskirts of Terracina. Due to the land's topography, the Battalion was subjected to deadly automatic fire. During the night, the enemy had brought up elements of another division to reinforce their position.

The next morning, the First Battalion discovered that Germans were positioned on the other side of a hill that they occupied. They retreated to a spot on a nearby hill and waited for the Third Battalion to be dispatched to the their weakened flank. At 1030, both battalions advanced inch by inch. The battle raged throughout the day. Late in the afternoon, the Second Battalion was called forward to relieve the battle-weary troops of the First, who rested in an area north of Fondi. The next objective for the 337th was to capture the city of Terracina.

Chapter 5:
Up Front

Editor's Note: *Unlike Byers' descriptive recollections of his state-side military service, he kept abbreviated notes about his time in Italy in pocket-sized pads. It was necessary to edit and refer to 337th Infantry Regiment's Monthly Reports to expand on the words he jotted down between marches and bomb blasts.*

May

May 19

Dear Mrs. L. & Janet -

"Up Front"

Just a few lines to let you know I'm all right. I guess the papers keep you well informed as the "Drive" progresses. It's been rough, but well worth while. The Yank dogfaces don't have to take off their hats off to anyone as fighters. They just won't be stopped by anything the Krauts throw at them. We got steak and fresh potatoes tonight. First hot meal since we started. Plenty of fleas, flies, and stench. Wow! The towns have taken a beating, but the people are glad to see us. Sure could go for a shower and clean clothes. We had little sleep and ate K Rations. How's Janny doing in school? She shouldn't have any trouble because she's very bright.

As Ever,
Don

The Regiment entered Formia on the 20th — it was nearly leveled. The townspeople spoke good English. The house where we stayed had a view of Gaeta. The next day, we passed through Itri on our way toward Fondi. A shell landed in back of us as we drove in our jeep, but no one was hurt. Itri was a shambles while Fondi's worst damage was a dismantled bridge. The townspeople were happy to see us. I got a close look at some of the prisoners.

On the 23rd, we moved north to Terracina which was in bad shape. Krauts were dug in under tombs which made it a tough fight. After a barrage, they would come out and man their guns in time to cut down the doggies (*Americans*). A cemetery on top of Hill 133 was our strong point, and they had perfect observation. We couldn't get around the road. An anti-tank gun had our tank divisions scared. One battalion managed to get around in back and the Jerries (*Germans*) pulled out. There were lots of pillboxes around and the Krauts left guns and equipment inside of them. During their retreat, the Germans flooded the marshes and vandalized the churches. On a stroll about town, we saw G.I.'s coming out of a cellar with helmets, cups, tubs, and everything imaginable filled with vino — dago red. We dug some wine out of the rubble. Pvt. Francis Shane got drunk and climbed on a Kraut anti-aircraft gun, then pointed it out to sea and was ready to fire it when someone stopped him. We stayed in a house on a mountainside.

The following day, the Colonel had the beach cleared of mines and we got our first bath in a long time. We walked through lanes of piled up mines to swim at the beach that was used by ancient Romans.

The Regiment went into reserve on the 27th to get rest and equipment after Sezze and Priverno fell. On the way there, we saw that the Krauts had flooded the Pontine Marshes that had been drained by Mussolini to provide more farmland. We went swimming in a lagoon. Afterward, we received orders to prepare for a move up to Velletri to relieve the 30th Infantry the next day.

On the 31st, we found out that Lt. Schumeister lost his way, went past us, and got caught up by the Krauts. We moved toward Lariano, but the town hadn't been cleaned out. We were held up by German snipers and tanks that blocked the road, so we sat in a barn next to a dead doggie. Suddenly, we saw some doggies come tearing down the hill from town. I asked one guy what was wrong, and he said, "Damned if I know. I'm just following the crowd." Just as we were trying to figure out what to do, some of our I&R Platoon came along and said that some Kraut tanks were loose and headed our way. We stayed there waiting for orders when the new Assistant Commanding Officer came flying past us — that was all we needed. The counterattack by the tanks made us run back to our old command post in a trench. The U.S. tanks were afraid. Back at the post, a former Kraut position, we caught our breath and the latest news.

Some of the fellows dug wine out of a cellar. Results: one drunk under arrest for bawling out the Commanding Officer and two dared each other to carry a wire into town without getting caught by Krauts. Staff Sgt. Lorenz "Momma Fix" Fix, a 6 footer, got wounded in town and was carried to safety by the smallest man in the company - 5'1".

June

The Regiment moved into an R&R Station at Monte Compatri on June 1. After setting up equipment, someone looking for loot discovered a Kraut in the cellar. An air raid was the featured attraction that night. Our mess tent finally caught up to us the next morning, so after a hot breakfast, we moved up to the Third Battalion's position. The troops were still driving on. The Division Commander Major Geneneral Coulter came up to see us; I guess he thought the Krauts were miles away. I was laying on the ground working the board when some Jerry shells came our way. There was one hole for six officers and as I looked across at them all I could see was legs. Oy, what a sight. Hot iron sure makes a man forget rank. After the shelling, we saw Krauts being booed by Dagoes along the road. Fascists tried to escape.

We left for Rome on the 3rd. A German sniper killed ten soldiers during the move. We marched under an ancient viaduct into Rome where the townspeople threw roses, clapped, and gave us wine and food. They put roses on dead G.I.s lying along the roads and in the fields. People hate Krauts and are tired of the war. People go back to their farming as soon as the front line troops pass — seemed very odd. We spent two nights in a house in a sort of development project in the suburbs of Rome. We flushed three snipers out of a nearby house.

The next morning, we loaded up, then waited all day. Some of us attended a festival before we all moved out in a convoy at dusk. We went one mile and waited at the main road for other convoys to pass. A Kraut plane strafed us. The first time I was in a hole, the second time I got caught in a truck. Lt. Col. Lauferski left us. He took off! We finally got to an old fort on the opposite side of town where we spent the night.

On the 8th, we moved twenty miles to a small lake near Monterosi, where we took a swim, then cooked a swell meal. The Lone Ranger still comes over the radio each night. There were lots of destroyed Kraut vehicles and equipment abandoned along the road. The bridges and parts of the town were mined. We slowly made our way through town then took Highway 2 toward Florence.

June 11

Dear Harry & Kate -

Just resting now after two months of chasing the Krauts. We're beside a lake, and a soft cool rain is pattering on the roof. A quiet Sunday after-noon. The coffee's boiling, and jam and crackers are waiting — G.I. style, of course. All we need is a radio. Just got some bread, too. It sure is swell to be able to sleep in peace at night with only a little bombing and strafing to bother us. I haven't seen Pete for a while, but I've talked to him over the phone. Rome sure is a beautiful city, and so are the girls. I had plenty of wine and ice cream — some combination — and the people wouldn't let us pay for it.

Love to all
- Don

We remained by the lake until noon on the 14th, when we received orders to move back through Rome along Route 8 and through Rallentare. We set up the switchboard in a house two miles from the ocean by Lido di Roma. It was a ghost town full of modern buildings, but it had booby traps and mines all over. We ate hot meals, slept, saw movies, U.S.O. shows, parades, and got passes. I visited Rome and saw most of the old ruins. St. Peter's Cathedral is beautiful and even a Methodist like myself didn't seem out of place. The mosaics and frescoes are gorgeous, and the statues are out of this world. I climbed to the top of the dome for a panoramic view of the "Eternal City." Vatican City is quite large, and the gardens are very lovely: flowers and ledges in religious designs, miniature waterfalls, and several shrines. The dome is some 600 feet high. Boy it's some climb. We hired a guide to show us the various mosaics and statues. The high arch — or is it altar? — is done in gold leaf and marble. The designs are exquisite. I also saw the Coliseum and the various tombs and arches. All cameras must be checked before you go in because no pictures can be taken inside. We've been catching up on sleep and food. I lost about ten to fifteen pounds. I'm living near a 15th Century castle in a house that has a toilet that flushes. Boy, is that a treat.

On July 14, we marched up Route 1 to Civitivechia, where we stopped for dinner. Afterward, I drove up the route to Grosetto then turned off in Rocostrada to set up the switchboard in a field. A few days later, our unit passed through Cecina and Saline, then halted in Volterra for five hours. We picked up some souvenirs before moving onto a new area. There were Kraut air raids on the nights of the 26th and 27th. The next day, we moved back through Cecina, Saline, and Volterra. There was a beautiful view of the rolling valleys and mountains with towns on top. Dagoes fear us. Two G.I.s raped a girl.

*Byers' Army-issue Thames
.32 caliber revolver.*

August

On August 14, we moved up to a big castle on 7,000 acres of ground. At the top of the castle there was a library with paintings and hundreds of books. We moved up on the line on the 16th. Krauts were positioned across the river. We came upon another old castle and searched the wine cellar, but the Dagoes took the wine out, so we couldn't drink it. In Gombassi, we were met by plenty of heavy shelling. The Battalion caught hell. On the 26th, we moved back and stopped in the woods five miles from Certaldo.

September

It rained very heavily from September 7 to 10. We got washed out and slept in a supply tent. The next day, we moved forward through Friani, San Pancraizio, and Casiano to Florence, which was very nice — a big town with pretty girls. The bridges were demolished. We moved onto Pratolina, then Fontebuono about two miles from the front. There were 240mm Howitzers all around, but no enemy artillery. Mule teams were at a command post that was setup in a house in the forest.

On the 13th, we moved up through San Pietro and crossed a smoked-out bridge. At last, we're up against the Gothic Line. We made a command post along a railroad. There was a tough fight up on the mountains with lots of our heavy artillery. The Krauts were dug in.

We moved up to Lucca, on the 15th, to a small hole on the side of a hill. The next day, we moved closer to the front, across a level valley up into the mountains where we saw tracers from our machine guns at night. Our boys have almost taken the objective. The First British Division was on our right with some Indian regiments. Our artillery was blasting constantly, but the Krauts were well dug in. The mountainsides were very rocky. First Lt. Clarence Guffey had an observation post in the Krauts' sector. We moved up as far as Guffey's observation post, on the 18th, but we couldn't move to the base of the mountain to get to Monte Pratone. The Krauts zeroed in on our path with mortars so we couldn't move. We set up a temporarily camp on top of a hill. The mule teams drew fire on us. The British were going to lay down a barrage to help us. I talked to some men from the Second Royal Scots. Nice fellows. It was cold at night which made it hard to operate the switchboard. We had a perfect view of our artillery.

The next day, we moved up the mountain to an 88th Division command post. On the way we crossed open ground and got light machine gun fire. The Krauts opened up on us. Four bursts! They fired too high. We ducked down off the road and cut through some woods toward a safe spot at a command post in a thick forest of pines. We moved out at twilight with a mule train and walked down the mountainside on a rough trail into the night. One mule fell off the trail, but it didn't get hurt. The command post was shelled heavily. We finally got to the bottom to Moscheta where we stayed in a church overnight. Rain came through holes in the roof. All of us were dead tired, hungry, and dirty. We ate some chicken the next morning. My left leg was in bad shape. Pvt. John Tarosky walked in this morning. Then at night the rear echelon operators came up.

On the 21st, the 88th Division moved in to relieve us during the night, but we had to stay there in reserve. The wiremen had a helluva job going up and down the trails with mules because it was still drizzling. Plenty of Kraut prisoners were coming in — a very sorry-looking lot.

At 0420 on the 23rd, we moved up to Firenzola then to Borgo San Lorenzo. We set up a temporary switchboard in the back end of a little house. The boys picked up pots and pans. Troops moved along Highway 65 until the Battalion came in contact with the enemy, so we settled down. At 0930, we moved along Highway 65 to San Pelligrino. The Colonel was five miles ahead. Krauts were sure pulling out fast. The radio was more useful than the wire — we couldn't keep the wire in. We were held up by German snipers at night on our way across the valley to a command post. We would be under direct observation in the day, but the trip was quiet. I felt scared when we first started, but I was okay after a hundred yards. We helped the Second Battalion operate. We stayed overnight in a house that was on top of a small hill in Visignano. Eight G.I.'s were dead in the next room.

The Krauts were putting up a lot of opposition. They fired three shells right at dawn on the 26th. I could hear guns, then shells land. It rained from the 27th to the 29th. The shelling finally stopped. The Krauts were pulling out. We were now in a stinky barn, but safe. It was warm at night and well blacked-out. My stomach was in bad shape. I had barely any water in my canteen, so I had to drink rain water while eating K Rations. The night before we had rabbit and chicken. Blankets were sent up to the boys on the front. There was rain and mud

The Gothic Line - Fall 1944

Ferrara

HWY 64

Bologna

HWY 65

Pistoia   Firenzuola

Gothic Line

Lucca   Prato   Florence

Pesaro

Pisa

Leghorn   Volterra

Siena

Grosseto

Viterbo   HWY 2

Civitacchia   Rome

The 85th Division advanced north for the Gothic Line. The German attacks and mountainous terrain were tough on the Allied Forces, but by the end of September, the Germans retreated to their next point of defense in Bologna.

* Above map based on maps printed in *The 85th Infantry Division in World War II* Schultz, Paul, L. (See **Bibliography** for more.)

everywhere. It was cold and damp. The next day, I shaved, washed my hands, and changed my socks for the first time since Moscheta. It was quiet there. Dagoes were stripping each other's houses bare, and each claimed the house belongs to him. I saw some pretty girls wandering around.

October

We took out the switchboard on the morning of October 1, then left the area by the afternoon. At 1530, we moved toward Piancaldo on a secondary road. We walked up a mountain and passed a house that was used as a pillbox. It contained dead Krauts and equipment. Over the crest to the road, we were under observation. We thumbed a ride to Rocco to get to a command post that was setup in a doctor's house in Piancaldo. It was very cold, and it rained the following day.

The rest of the command post moved up on the 3rd, but the doctor made me stay back until I got over my G.I. Blues. Three days later, I left Piancaldo for the next command post. I still felt weak. All of the rain made the trails very muddy and rough. There were lots of mines. Two medic jeeps and a tank hit mines. The command post was in a farm house. I got a new pair of boots and a jacket. The weather was terrible on the 10th — it was very cold and windy with rain showers. We ate hot meals and slept. It sure helped a lot. A lot of the boys have colds or the G.I. Blues.

October 11 was my birthday — thirty years. I'd sure like to push it back ten. The following day, we pulled out the switchboard and moved up to Cadi Lavacchio, located along a riverbed. We stayed down in a house's cellar. I had a beautiful view of the mountains and was able to see an air corp bomb a castle that was being used by the Jerries.

The Regiment was pulled off the line on the 12th to rest for several days. Tarosky went to the hospital for a fever and the chills. Packages were finally coming in. Bob Ramsey (a *friend from back home*) stopped over on the 16th. Pete and I had a nice chat with him and took some pictures of the three of us. We needed showers and clean clothes. Some boys went to Florence on pass.

October 19

Dear Harry -

Looks like no turkey this year for Christmas unless it's out of a can. I've been reading about defense workers who are leaving their war jobs to go back to their pre-war jobs. They sure are confident, but I think a few days up here with us would convince them that the war still goes on. Especially when they hear the shells and see and smell the dead. I saw Bob Ramsey the other day. We always have a nice chat about things and people we know back home. He's a nice fellow. Tell Kate I often dream about her coconut pie!

Love to all,
Don

We really had a "hot breakfast" on the 20th
— four shells landed in front of the command
post. We ate outside and shrapnel hit the wall
where we ate, so we moved inside. Shells
landed about twenty yards away. We were lucky.
All day and night the Germans shelled the bridge
behind us, but they didn't hit us. They did manage to knock out vehicles, mules, men, and
lines. We set up the switchboard that afternoon.

On the 23rd, we pulled out the switchboard,
then took off for a forward position on the side
of a hill. The roads were very bad and vehicles
got stuck and went off the sides of the road.
In the afternoon, we started for the next command post and got stuck. Capt. Speck got scared
and took off and left us. We finally got the jeep
out then it got stuck again. We eventually
reached the Second Battalion's position where we
spent the night. The following morning, a few of
us left for a command post that was setup in a
pink church. It was some damn climb — mud all the
way and up the hill.

The Germans really started bombing the place
on the 26th. Shells landed on all sides of us.
We didn't bother going to chow. It was a half-
a-mile to the kitchen, and the road was all
exposed. Too damn close! A mortar shell hit the
side of the church and wounded some men. They
must have us zeroed in. Tarosky came back from
the hospital; he looked bad.

Dear Harry et al -

We're still in the mountains, mud, and rain. I got the carton of cigs in a box Mother sent. Thanks very much. If it wasn't silly, I'd tell you that I'm saving them for a rainy day. Haven't heard from Bob Ramsey for a while - don't expect to see him either. Not up here at least. I guess we'll have C Rations instead of turkey this year; still, I guess that is more than some people will eat. Tell Kate I'm still looking forward to that coconut pie. And how! I hope I can pick up some Christmas presents, but if I can't I'm sure you will understand.

Love to all,
Don

There was still plenty of shelling on November 1, but not as much the following day. Thank heaven! On the 4th, a plane strafed the artillery behind us, but our anti-aircraft chased it away. We were still getting shells and mortar fire.

The Regiment reached Purrochia di Sassimo on the 9th. The Limeys relieved us — now for a rest. The next morning, I woke up to see snow on the ground. It was a pretty sight, just enough to cover the ground. We moved toward St. Lucia, then turned left. Kraut pillboxes were dug into the hills along Highway 65. The Jerries had a swell field of fire and observation. The highway was like one long tank trap. It was amazing how we ever took those mounts.

Unbelievable. We stayed in a very large barn. I saw a bull and cow mate. The rest of the Division arrived at 0100 on the 12th. It was a nice quiet Sunday spent working on the equipment, then a quick half-a-mile hike to chow. Days later, we marched north to Pistoia then moved off the line to Gagliano. I was granted a four-day pass to Rome on the 27th. It was a heavenly time.

December

I returned from Gagliano on December 2. I received a letter from Sally Yarnell, a nurse who I had met from the American Red Cross. For most of the month, the Regiment rested and relieved other units. On the 23rd, we left in a hurry for Lucca because the Krauts were supposed to be attacking the 92nd Infantry Division in the Serchia Valley sector. It was merely small patrols, but the boys from the 92nd panicked and fell back several miles. British and Indian soldiers relieved the 92nd and took back the ground without a fight.

There was a big party for the brass on Christmas Eve. We had a few drinks, too. On Christmas Day, we had a big roast turkey dinner with mashed potatoes, green peas, dressing, giblet gravy, cranberry sauce, and apple pie. I got 8 boxes in the mail. We're still on a half-an-hour alert.

A Christmas postcard Byers sent to his parents. The American Red Cross printed these cards for soldiers to send holiday greetings to their friends and family back home.

Chapter 6:
Mud, Rain, and Cold With No Sleep

1945

January

The Regiment was on a two-hour alert on New Year's Day. We had a big meal again: turkey. There were olive orchards all around the castle where we were staying in Lorenzo Moriano. Pete is now a staff sergeant. Sally Yarnell called me from Florence on January 2. We moved back to Gagliano on the 6th, and setup in the stud farm again. The townspeople were glad to see us. It snowed the next day.

We pulled out on the 9th, for the same place where we left the front at the pink church. It was just a few of us who took the cold nervous ride. The roads were in good condition. At 1400, we arrived at the foot of the hill. The river bottom was full of equipment. Speck went up to learn the score. We were still waiting by 1700 and there was no place to stay down there. Finally, we called him and he told us to move up. A British division made a new path that was much steeper, but it was shorter and better for walking. It was very quiet all the way up. Pete met me and got me a space in a chapel where he was staying with some British troops. The Limeys were very friendly and obliging — and I was just in time for hot tea.

The next day, we were still waiting around. Pvt. Kenton Nelsen went up to the First Battalion to put up a switchboard. I sure caught up on my tea. We had tea four times daily. Molte good. We had no rations of our own, so the Limeys fed us. We took our switchboard to a dugout on the side of a hill on the 11th. It was all setup when Pvt. John Sullivan finally got there and things started to straighten out. Snow covered everything in sight, and it was cold as hell. Late at night, I listened to the radio via a hook-up with almost everyone in the 88th Division. All the boards were listening to music. It snowed for days. Bob Ramsey stopped by on the 15th.

A few days later, we moved into an old dilapidated house in Purrochia di Sassimo. It was so bad that we had to put up wooden doors, cover the floor, fix the stove, and put mud and canvas inside cracks in the walls. We brewed tea on the night shift. Capt. Albert Nelson came back from the hospital. It snowed the next few days along with strong winds. I had some P.X. candy and three cans of beer.

On the 26th, rockets went overhead and landed behind us. It sounded like a train derailed. A large fire fight ensued on our left flank. The next day, I got a hot shower and clean clothes at the foot of the hill. I picked up a carton of Camels that Sally mailed to me. Planes were active during the night. Pfc. John Greer came back from the hospital on the 30th. He looked good. We didn't get any snow, but there was plenty of fog.

February

It was payday on February 1, so I sent home forty dollars. The conditions were very foggy and muddy. On the 6th, we saw two shells land and burst at the bottom of the hill. It killed one and wounded one. I received a box from home on the 8th. It rained the following day, but then it turned into snow while we worked on the hut. Several shells hit a hundred yards away. Eight of our high-velocity artillery shells burst overhead. Tarosky left on a pass on the 11th. I led the song service at church. The weather was nice for a change.

February 18

Dear Harry et al -

Evidently the people at home are all mixed up about what we are fighting for. Probably because they can't see clearly with the flag being waved in front of their faces, and the "hot air" and martial music. A couple of weeks in mud, rain, and cold with no sleep and hard rations would give them a different point of view. Some day I'll tell you all about it - when we get back our freedom of speech. Right now the Army forbids certain things. I haven't told Mother where I am because I don't want her to worry, so don't let on. Clare Luce seems to be the only one who realizes there is still a war in Italy. The Krauts are still throwing stuff at us.

As usual
- Don

I got a package with a book for Pete on the 19th. The next day, a 120mm mortar shell hit the First Battalion's command post, killing seven and wounding twelve soldiers. High-velocity artillery shells burst overhead later in the day. The Krauts pumped in about sixty to seventy shells during the evening on the 22nd. They were really close, with some landing in back of us and on both sides.

We watched the mountain to our left rear take a terrific pounding from a self-propelled gun on the morning of the 28th. It sounded so close, but the shots missed the houses. The firing continued into the night. At 2300, four self-propelled guns opened up and fired in three concentrations of at least a hundred shells each. Ninety percent of the shells went over the ridge into the valley. The barrage lasted until 0115.

March

On March 1, I received two boxes in the mail: a camera and pictures of my folks. Right before dusk, a self-propelled gun fired about two hundred rounds at some vehicles driving on a road along a ridge. The next day, we went up to the Regiment operation point to take pictures. It was some climb. The boys were dug in on all sides. The path was partly under observation. The valley was smokey. I took some snaps and looked through a scope at the ground and hills in front of us.

There was some heavy shelling on the morning of the 3rd. The sound of a self-propelled gun woke me up. Almost a direct hit on the rear board in the valley. It snowed during the night.

The British relieved us on the 11th, so we went back to Gagliano. After three days, half of the Company went to Montecatini for a rest. When they came back, the rest of us went to a small health resort. We lived in hotels and went to sulfur baths. The town was jammed with G.I.s, but there was not much doing. I went into Florence with Capt. Nelson and saw Sally for a few hours on the 20th. The next day, we caught a hop in and spent the day with Sally. When I returned, I was yanked out to Pisa, then sent to Arno for special river crossing training at a big staging area. I went back to Montecatini on the 27th to complete my pass, but there was still nothing to do except watch movies and take baths.

On the 30th, we left for a new area and stopped at a big house in town. There were lots of pretty girls — molte bino. We played lots of ball and had plenty of vino. The weather was swell and the people were very nice. The town had the prettiest girls I have seen yet. Two G.I.s found a "private" whore — the whore not so private now. Colonel Hughes played volleyball. The Headquarters Company volleyball team was the best in the Regiment. I went to a bar with a fellow corporal where we met four girls. We took a radio and danced. They spoke little English, but they were good dancers.

April

Our orders were to pull out at 2100 on April 1, and go north up along Highway 64, then cross a bridge. Big stuff started hitting. We took shelter in a big house near the crossroads. The closest hit landed a hundred yards away. We were all scared and shaky. We finally pulled out and ran for it. We reached a command post area around 0200. No one was sure where it was — as usual. Morano was the last town we went through last night. The roads were choked and we had to hike to the top of a mountain to reach the next command post. We didn't arrive until 1445. I was able to fit in two hours of sleep.

April 14

Hi Harry -

Can't understand why you keep that old Stanley-Steamer. Why don't you junk it? As for jobs, how long did I roam around and then get slapped in the Army before I could settle into anything? Everyone talks about the things they're going to do for "our boys." Mealy-mouthed, cliché-spouting, so-called patriots make me sick in the stomach. None of us over here want any part of flag-waving or pretty speeches from anyone. Just give us the equipment. We'll take it from there.

Love to Nancy & Kate,
Don

We left for Vignola at noon on the 18th. There were lots of shell holes and dead mules along the way. There wasn't any German resistance. Things were all confused. We left the area at 1300 for San Pietro. We had a good view of the 10th Mountain Division's sector. There were plenty of dugouts that were fixed up swell. I got a full night's sleep at a house on top of a hill. The following day, Sullivan and I moved forward, but snipers blocked the road. We were pinned down and unable to move forward to the next command post until 0130. After noon, we left for the forward post and didn't get shot at. We watched a battle take place upon a hill in front of us. The Krauts put up a stiff resistance. The rest of the command post went to Agato once the hill was taken while we moved up to Gesso before night fall. The next day, we pulled out at 1100. The roads were choked with vehicles. We found some wine and spent the night in a nearby town called Fray.

All of us were awakened at 0400 on the 22nd and given orders to leave the area and join two of our battalions to form a task force in Montirone. Once the place was secured, the townspeople emerged to hand out vino, bread, and eggs. We got held up in Camposanto where the task force was fighting to cross the river. G.I.s swam across the water to cut down demolition charge wires strung on the bridge. We crossed in back of tanks, then went into parts of town before anyone else. The townspeople said that a German armored car left five minutes before we arrived. The people cried and kissed us. Early the next day, we left for a new command post. The Krauts strafed the roads with three planes. Speck lost the convoy ahead. We went to the wrong place. Krauts were on the run again. Second Battalion took a German corps headquarters at 1700 and captured forty prisoners. The boys have reached the Po River. The 10th Mountain Division crossed the water and found Kraut bridges. In the nearby town of Quistello there was a Kraut hospital with patients, staff, and ambulances. The Regiment took lots of prisoners and vehicles. I setup the command post and got ready to cross the following day. The boys in town got all the pistols, cameras, etc.

A battle to cross the Po River jumped off at 0530 on the 24th. Our orders were to move up to the river's edge. After a big barrage, troops went over without any resistance. At 0945, we paddled across the river carrying the switchboard — it was tough. We walked two miles, and on the way we met two Italians and got them to carry the board. We moved into a town called Sustinento. Our artillery killed two civilians and wounded eighteen. The only damage to the town was by us, but it wasn't too bad. There was no on else but us in the town. The Krauts pulled out two days ago except for twenty men who left last night. We stayed in Sustinento and found some good vermouth and lots of eggs. There was bombing and strafing on the other side of the Po.

We pulled out at 0830 on the 26th for Ferrara. The Vigasio Mountains were in sight. We stopped to eat lunch then headed toward Verona. At Castel D' Azzano, we stopped to rest at a big old castle which had some pianos inside. By 1630, we reached Verona and met up with the Second Battalion. We stayed there for a few days until the 30th. At 2000, officers ordered us to pull out and head east across railroad yards that were blown to hell. The tracks and cars were in all shapes and directions and the buildings were rubble. Parts of the town were in bad shape and several bridges were knocked out. There was a large swift river nearby. On up the road, we stopped because our orders changed. We spent the night in the next town, Vicenza. It was strictly fascist.

May

Three thousand Kraut prisoners were taken into custody on May 1. Our group left town at 1245 with the Second Battalion ahead of us. We passed through San Pietro, Fontaniva, Cittadella, and Bassano. They ran into a firefight. There were plenty of partisans. And the prettiest girls I'd seen in Italy. Many blondes. We moved through Treviso and Cornedo before stopping in Fenner for the night. Fenner seemed to be a health resort. The next morning, part of the Regiment went forward going up into the Alps. Houses were stuck way up on the mountains. The weather was cold. We headed for Belluno, then took a right turn toward Busche, then San Giustina. There was some mix-up ahead. A corps of Krauts wanted to quit or armistice. Colonel Hughes said "as prisoners of war only." After lunch, we headed for Susins, a town on the side of a mountain. The partisans were very strong and organized. The townspeople were nice to us. Someone handed me a dozen eggs.

The War was over in Italy! We had numbers of German divisions cut off and surrendering.

337th's Advances in Italy by May 1945

Austria

X Belluno

Feltre

Vincenza   Treviso

Verona

Padoua   Venice

Po River

Ferrara   Po Line

Modena   Bologna

After their landing in Naples, the 337th Regiment traveled more than 400 miles in jeeps, tanks, and on foot scaling mountains and crossing rivers to defeat the Nazis. They reached Belluno and were poised to cross the border into Austria when Germany officially surrendered on May 8, known as VE Day (Victory in Europe).

* Above map based on maps printed in **The 85th Infantry Division in World War II** Schultz, Paul, L. (See **Bibliography** for more.)

I set up the switchboard in a hotel named Albergo Alpino at 0430 on the 3rd. Boys talking on the radio said there would be a big conference here in the morning. A Kraut commanding general of the 278th Infantry Division and his staff met General Coutler, Colonel Hughes, and a Corps Chief of Staff. There were still some German divisions who wouldn't quit. Hughes sure made some tough terms. The Krauts poured into the camp all day and night.

The conference was between a German army general and our our commanding officers. The Krauts called off hostilities in some places. Tarosky finally made rotation and left the next morning. The kid sure is happy. It was damn cold. I drank coffee while working on the board at night. The boys on the radio said that the Krauts have quit in Holland, Denmark, and north-western Germany. There weren't too many left. It was announced that peace would be official at midnight on May 8. I didn't feel any different. The next day, I got a Kraut switchboard, then had to go to a nearby town to get parts from the 76th Panzer Corps. The Krauts then went to Belluno with Speck. It was a swell ride. The Third Battalion moved 55 miles away from us on the 10th. I was using Kraut circuits now. The following day, we passed through Mesa on our way to join the First Battalion headed for Belluno.

Susins, Italy

Dear Folks -

As you can see, I made it to the end in one piece. And I've thanked Him for it, too.

Our main topic now is "What next?" But after the things we've seen and done, it can't be any worse.

We're in a pretty little mountain village high up above a river. It's very beautiful — now that we can relax enough to enjoy it.

The Kraut prisoners have been rounded up, searched, and sent to the rear; so now we can catch up on food and sleep. There is a lake a few miles away so some of the boys have been swimming, but I think I'll wait until it gets a little warmer. The water up here is as clear as glass, the beds are white sand and pebbles. Very pretty. I've been taking pictures, but I can't get enough film.

Don't forget to keep me informed on the progress of your business venture. I know it will be a success, so stop pacing the floor at night.

The censorship ban has been lifted, so get out your maps of northern Italy. Put your finger on Verona then trace a line on up to Bassano, Feltre, then Belluno. Halfway between Feltre and Belluno you'll find our present location.

Every day more of the boys are getting "rejection slips" from their girls at home. They couldn't wait. And lots of the married men are having wife troubles. Lucky me with no worries at all.

Regards to the whole family.

Love,
Don

There was an officers dance on the 12th. I sat by the window. Lots of people gave me drinks of cognac, champagne, and vermouth. An officer sent us to his room for some U.S. Whiskey. Some partisans were there too. The girls were not too slick; most of them came for the eats. They sure were a scream — comic opera heroes. We moved to a resort by a lake on the 14th. I rode up to the Third Battalion, through Belluno, and up a highway to Piave. The scenery was beautiful as we rode through the mountains on a road that followed the river. The grass looked like velvet. At noon, we had peach ice cream.

Editor's Note: *Byers' battlefield notes end as of May 14, so his letters and excerpts from the 337th Infantry Regiment Monthly Reports are used to track his activities from this point forward.*

As of May 15, the Regiment occupied areas in and around Belluno. The remainder of the month was spent disarming and evacuating German troops in their sector. The 337th was assigned to supervise the 76th Panzer Corps surrender of more than 20,000 troops and 500 vehicles. The orders were to evacuate the enemy prisoners to Bassano, a task that was expected to take several days to complete. The massive convoy moved south on the 18th toward Mas for a German ammunition assembly point where the enemy would unload their surrendered equipment and weapons. At one point during the unpacking, a great explosion shook the ground. Tons of ammunition ignited damaging the assembly point and killing an American and ten Germans.

The Regiment arrived in Bassano on the 26th where they handed over the prisoners to elements of the Italian Folgore Group (partisans). The 337th was relieved of all military duties and the partisans assumed control of the zone. The last days of May were spent relaxing. All battalions conducted solemn memorial services to honor the men who had given their lives in the Italian campaigns. The battalions were dispersed throughout the area, some stayed in Belluno, others were sent to Agordo, and the special companies went to Lake Alleghe. The entire 85th Division was relieved on the 28th.

June 3

Alleghe, Italy

Dear Mrs. Lewis & Janet -

Just got back from a visit to Leghorn. We drove about 350 miles non-stop to get there. And when our business was finished, some of the boys set up rum and Cokes for us. And did we enjoy it.
I only have 72 points, so it will be some time before I get out. We are sending home a lot of men over 40-years-old or with 85 points and over.
But they — the Army — don't give the infantry any credit for combat time.
My regards to Herman and the family.

Love,
Don

In less than a month, the 85th evacuated nearly 30,000 prisoners. "Custer's Division" now rested in the vicinity of Feltre and Belluno to await further orders. For a brief period, it was on alert because of a dispute over the occupation of Trieste between partisans and forces of the Yugo-Slav National Liberation Army.

Soldiers who were eligible for discharge under the Advanced Service Rating Score point system returned to the United States. ASRS was a scoring system used by the military to determine which soldiers went home first. At the end of the war in Europe, a total of 85 points were required for a soldier to return to the States. Troops who had less than 85 continued to serve in Europe as an occupying force or were shipped to the Pacific to fight the Japanese. Soldiers earned points based on their length of service (+1 for each month); overseas service (+1 for each month); any decorations they were awarded (+5); campaign stars worn on theater ribbons (+5); and for each of their children under the age of 18 (+12 for up to 3 children). Officers were now busy organizing discharges and transfers instead of battle strategies. (ASRS as described on www.custermen.com)

Soldiers who were not yet eligible for discharge lingered around Belluno waiting for the orders to go home or be redeployed to the Pacific Theatre to finish off the Japanese. The wire corps maintained the lines of communication between the 85th Division's battalions using only the essential equipment necessary to do so. The men also spent the month relaxing between light training that emphasized orientation and education. The troops spent the 22nd at the Belluno airstrip for a field day of athletics, military events, and horse racing. All the 337th's companies competed against each other, with H Company winning most of the events. The following day, the 85th was ordered to prepare to move to the Volturno Redeployment Training Area near Caserta. The 337th boarded trains or jumped into trucks headed for Volturno while skeleton crews of communication teams remained behind.

July

The Division's move to Caserta was completed by mid-month. Col. Hughes was transferred to the 5th Army Headquarters. Light training continued with the emphasis on military courtesy, close-order drills, interior guard duty, and award ceremonies. Men with enough points were sent home while the others waited to reach 85. A liberal pass policy allowed soldiers to visit Rome, Naples, and other cities for days at a time. It was apparent that the 85th was no longer needed in Italy, and word was received that it would return to the States in the near future for demobilization.

August

The war against the Japanese in the Pacific Theatre was fierce, but the Allies were making headway. They gained footholds by taking island after island, stepping closer to Japan. American B-29 planes dropped the first atomic bombs used in warfare on Hiroshima and Nagasaki killing almost 135,000. The Japanese were under-supplied, overwhelmed, and could not withstand another atomic attack. They were the only remaining member of the Axis, so they had no other choice but to surrender to the Allies on August 9th. The U.S. military's point system was suspended shortly after the surrender. Through the entire war, the 85th Division suffered about 7,000 casualties (with 1,700 Killed in Action) of its force of more than 15,000 men.

More and more American G.I.s were sent home each day. The 337th was ordered to close out of

Leghorn, Italy

Dear Elizabeth & Janet -

I'm still in Italy waiting for Uncle Sam to decide just what to do with me. By the looks of things, I'll be here a few more months. But I don't mind because I know I'll get home some day, and in one piece, too.

The weather was unbearably hot during July, but it has turned cold and rainy now. Soon the miserable Italian fall and winter will be on us. I've been getting a lot of sun and exercise at our bathing beach.

How's my favorite blonde these days? I hope she's looking forward to school this fall. I guess she'll be too big to hold on my lap when next I see her.

Lots of the boys are leaving every day for home. So maybe one of these days...

When the news of Japan's surrender came over the radio, I started ducking because some of the boys got some ammunition for their guns. What a wild night! But I guess we were entitled to a little hell raising.

It's time for me to go to work now. Yep, even on Sundays.

My regards to the whole family,
Don

the Volturno RTA on the 14th, to prepare for their return to Naples...where their gallant fight against the Nazis had begun. Byers received his last pay as an active soldier and packed a few souvenirs. On the 16th, soldiers were assembled for a brief farewell ceremony on the dock before they boarded the USS West Point bound for home. As the ship slowly departed, Don stood smoking on the bow reminiscing about his first steps in Italy. The crashing sounds of bomb blasts still echoed in his ears. His eyes remembered the final expressions on the faces of dead soldiers. Some memories he would keep, while others were flicked into the Mediterranean Sea like a cigarette butt...drifting on top of the water until the waves finally consumed it.

Chapter 7:
Going Home

August 1945

It had been more than a week since the 337th left Naples aboard the USS West Point. The men were eager to get home and the ship just never seemed to move fast enough. A roar of shouts and whistles filled the morning air when the American shores appeared to them in the distance.

The ship docked at Hampton Roads in Virginia where the men were ushered onto trains headed for Camp Patrick Henry. Troops were assigned a barracks, allowed to shower, and issued clean uniforms before chow. Everything was by the numbers, all together and at the same time once again.

The soldiers returned to their quarters after dinner where they waited to be dismissed. It seemed to them that would be the next logical step. Rumors passed from man to man, but Byers had learned not to believe everything that he heard.

An officer entered the barracks and ordered the men to assemble for a meeting. They stood at attention as they were praised for their gallant service and informed that the 337th Infantry Regiment would be officially deactivated at 2400 on August 26.

But as formal as their induction, so was their separation from the Army. A series of paperwork and examinations had to be completed before the men could leave the base. Those who hailed from Virginia would be home in days, while the remaining personnel were transferred to military reception stations closer to their homes. It wasn't until the middle of September that Don was sent to the Separation Center #45 at Fort Indiantown Gap in central Pennsylvania.

Don spent a few weeks in domestic service at the military reservation while he hoped to return to Philadelphia before his 31st birthday, but to his dismay he was forced to celebrate yet another birthday as an enlisted man. It wasn't until October 14 that he was honorably discharged with decorations that included a bronze star, a good conduct medal, and the combat infantry badge for his heroic, exemplary service during combat. After three and a half years, Don's American Odyssey was over.

He told his family the good news, so they planned to meet him at the train station and cook a grand welcome home dinner - no doubt it was the best meal he'd had in years.

After the meal, he was handed a letter from Ann. It had been rerouted when the military realized that he was back in the States. This letter was much different from her last. She welcomed him home with light-hearted jokes and news about some of their mutual friends. She hoped to see him soon and signed the letter "Lots of Love, Ann." It took a few minutes for him to decide how to react. He remembered the heartbreaking "Dear John Letter" she sent him before he shipped out to Africa. A lot of the soldiers had a girl back home to dream about when things got rough, but Don had no one. He wondered if they would pick things up where they left off in 1943. But their love was yet another casualty of the war.

It's unknown if Don kept in contact with Sally Yarnell, the American Red Cross nurse he befriended while in Italy. As with many overseas love affairs during World War II, they ended once soldiers and nurses received orders to return home.

Although Don was not home for his birthday, he would be home for the holidays. He was delighted by the thoughts of spending Thanksgiving and Christmas in a warm home rather than in a damp drafty castle. He would not only give thanks to God for the feast, but for his life. The Christmas presents he bought were to thank his family for all the cards and gifts they had sent to him not only on Christmas, but year round. This New Year's Eve would be spent looking forward to infinite possibilities instead of an imaginative question mark.

October 23

At Home

Dear Elizabeth & Janet -

I'm beginning to get used to civilian life again. Kinda tough, what with rationing, etc. But I think I'm going to like it in this country. Honest!

Yep, I'm just plain Mr. again. I still can't believe it, though.

It's been a long time since I heard from you. How's the business venture? And my best girl, how is she? Does she like school?

So far, I haven't thought about going to work. Just laying around taking things easy. Catching up on food, sleep & laughter occupies most of my time.

The rest of the time is spent dodging girls with matrimony on their minds. Most of them seem to think that a kiss means wedding bells. Up to this date I've been able to out-talk and out-run them. But one never knows.

I'd like to know what my favorite blonde wants from Santa this year. Maybe I can make a deal with him. I guess dolls are things of the past now?

My family is naturally happy and content now. Although they'd like me to stay home more, they realize that I'm restless and find it hard to stay in any one place for very long.

Hope to hear from you soon,
Don

As the year turned from 1945 to 1946, Don returned to his church's choir and also got a job as a shipping clerk with Fairmount Motor Products. He enjoyed the work. It wasn't too demanding but his body would get sore from spending so much time on his feet. The old back injuries he suffered while he was a soldier worsened so he saw a doctor who prescribed medicine for the aches, but the pain always returned. The job at Fairmount was going well, but Don knew that if he had some type of college degree he'd be in a better position for a promotion, hopefully a nice desk job. He decided to take night courses to be certified in Traffic Control for Motor Freight at Temple University.

He found time for dates on the weekends, but he kept women at arm's length. He saw Ann from time to time, but they merely exchanged friendly greetings. A friend, Art Dineen, arraigned a blind date for Don with Ruth Sands, a girl who worked with him at Penn Mutual Life Insurance. Ruth was a divorcee who moved to Philadelphia to live with her uncle within the past year. That fact didn't bother Don, but he thought it might make his parents a bit leery of her. The date with Ruth was repeatedly postponed for one reason or another, so he didn't meet her until a holiday dance for Penn Mutual's employees. They enjoyed each other's company at the party and agreed on another date.

Now a year after he returned from the war, Don had a job, was enrolled in college, and was dating a girl. 1947 was bound to be a good year.

The weekdays were tough for Don because of the demands of work and school. He worked during the day at Fairmount, then attended a couple night classes at Temple. Although the last class he attended was four years ago in the Army, he enjoyed learning, which reflected in his admirable grades. Between work, college, and his involvement at church, he had little time to loaf.

Don called Ruth regularly, but they generally met on the weekends for movies, dinner, or an occasional Philadelphia Eagles game. The way she hollered at the opposing team and cheered for the home team amused him. As the weeks past, Don became more and more interested in Ruth and he believed it was time for his parents to meet her. He decided to introduce her to them over a casu-

al Sunday dinner. He met Ruth at the train station a few blocks from his home. She was a bit nervous, so he tried to assure her that it would be fine. As they walked down the sidewalk, a bird dropped some irony on Ruth, staining the front of her light-colored blouse. They tried to clean the blouse the best they could, but the mark was still visible. She was afraid that it would ruin her chance to make a good first impression. When the two arrived at the Byers home, she bashfully mentioned the embarrassing blotch and to her surprise, George and Adela chuckled at the bird's sense of timing rather than the stain.

By the spring, the relationship between Don and Ruth was becoming stronger. He bought an engagement ring and proposed to Ruth after they dined to celebrate her 34th birthday on April 14. The failure of her first marriage lingered in his mind, but Don was confident that she knew that he would never betray her trust. She tearfully accepted his proposal and was thankful that she was able to find love once again when some people never experience it once in their lives. They married months later in September and honeymooned in Atlantic City.

Upon their return, Don and Ruth lived with his parents while they contemplated buying their own home. Don finished his studies at Temple and received certification in traffic control. He then decided to become a Master Mason at Frankford Lodge 292. His father was a Mason, as was his grandfather, so Don wanted to continue the family tradition.

Don was looking forward to settling into his own home now that he had earned a degree, secured a good job, and was married. But his culminating plans were changed when Ruth's mother suffered a debilitating stroke, so they decided to go to northeastern Pennsylvania to take care of her. The small city atmosphere of Wilkes-Barre was quite a change from bustling Philadelphia, but Don believed it would be a better place to raise a child whenever that day arrived. He quickly became involved in the choir at nearby Firwood United Methodist Church and attended the Caldwell Consistory in Bloomsburg, to further his Masonic degree. Although Ruth worked at a downtown bank, it was difficult for Don to find a job besides factory work.

He was still suffering back pain and was receiving outpatient treatment that only temporarily relieved the pain. He complained to doctors about constant aches in his lower back, soreness when bending, and that cold, damp weather seemed to intensify the pain. Don's physical ailments continued, which he expressed during a doctor's visit in April:

"In the latter part of 1942, while stationed at Camp Shelby, I first had trouble with my back. The climate was very damp, and I went to see the medics about it. They strapped me up. After this time, when it was my duty to lift anything heavy or stoop, I could feel that my back was really being strained. The damp weather, while stationed in Italy, made my back worse. Since discharge, I've had several treatments from the VA. Presently, my back bothers me more severely during damp weather. At times, it is very difficult for me to get myself out of bed; I have to have assistance. If I sit, walk, lie, or stand for any length of time, my back bothers me. I am employed as a gasoline station attendant and I will have to give up this type of work because of my condition.

I felt that being I was on my feet the biggest part of the day, that had something to do with the pain in my back. For the past three or four weeks, because of the damp weather, I seem to have been bothered more severely with the pain in my back. The pain generally starts in the lower part of my back, goes over to each hip and pain radiates down both legs. At the present time I am not working; I was laid off."

Eventually, doctors diagnosed his ailment as arthritis, and the Army awarded Don limited monetary compensation for his injuries. But it was not enough for the married couple to live on solely, so Don found work as a janitor at the nearby VA Hospital. In time, the physical demands of that job were too much for him to manage.

But Don was about to get some good news. In the spring of 1951, Ruth announced that she was pregnant. The anticipation of a son prompted him to become a scoutmaster for Boy Scout Troop 55 at Firwood. He was glad to be part of the organization he enjoyed as a child and wanted to share the group's survival and moral lessons with neighborhood youth and hopefully a son. But to his surprise the couple's first child was a girl, Ann Elizabeth, who was born on November 11. The couple was overjoyed by the birth as were his parents since Don was their only child.

It's not known whether the decision to name the child Ann was a point for arguement (considering that that was the name of the woman Don dated for a few years before he met Ruth). A safe assumption would be that they were more concerned with the situation at hand.

At first, Ann's health seemed fine until a few months later when a lump was discovered near her buttocks. They took Ann to the pediatrician for an examination, at which time the lump was diagnosed as spina bifida - a spinal defect. The condition is caused by several vertebrae in the spine that don't completely develop and enclose the spinal cord. A section of the cord protrudes out of the resulting gap in the spine and creates a bulge in the victim's back. Spina bifida can cause disabilities that vary from a lack of feeling in the lower part of the body to permanent paralysis. The bulge in a victim's back can be eliminated by surgery in which the spinal cord is buried deeper. Surgeons insert a tube into the cerebral ventricles where it's harmlessly absorbed. Physical therapy can strengthen leg muscles and enable many patients to eventually walk unaided or with braces.

Don and Ruth opted for the surgery which was scheduled for May 24. The couple consoled each other as they waited for the doctors to return with their prognosis. The doctors reported that they removed a tumor then found a suspicious growth at the base of the infant's spine. The outlook was grim. Ann spent several days in a recovery room, but eventually her small body couldn't withstand the immense physical stress of the surgery, and she died nine days later.

Death was something Don hadn't faced in several years. This time it was not a comrade in arms; someone he could mourn and then march past. Some people might have questioned why God had taken their child, but he knew that this misfortune was the Lord's will. He accepted Ann's death knowing that her future would have been painful and short-lived with her finally succumbing to the disease.

Dear Elizabeth et al -

The letters - such as your wonderful one - and other expressions of sympathy from our friends helped immeasurably to steady us. So many folks who were just acquaintances went out of their way to comfort us.

Naturally, our faith was terribly shaken, but our parents, by putting our roots in church at an early age, gave us bedrock to help us hold fast.

Now that we have had time to think and to learn what might have been in store for Ann, we know that His decision was wise. We loved her too much to see her suffer for who knows how long.

Ann was born with a simple fatty tumor on her left buttock. Last month, our family doctor suggested that we take her to a specialist on that type of thing. The surgeon suggested that we do it soon, before she became old enough to miss us while she would be in the hospital, and before she would begin to notice pain.

So, on May 24th we took her to the hospital. Our family doctor was assisting and he considered it so simple an operation that he didn't bother to wash up. When they removed the fatty tumor, they discovered a growth at the base of the spine. It came out of the spine through a bone separation.

That made it a very serious case. They did what seemed best and then we could only wait. There isn't too much they can do in a case such as Ann's. She came out of ether and was fine on Saturday, Sunday, and Monday, but Tuesday she started to slip. Then she'd have a good day, fol-lowed by a bad one.

Finally on Sunday evening when we were there, I called the nurse because I didn't like the way she looked. They put her in oxygen and called the doctor. He prescribed medicine, but he told me that there was nothing else that could be done.

She fought on through Sunday — Dad's birthday

— but Monday night at 5:30 p.m., she slipped away. That's just about the whole story.

We've been through a lot, but no more that many others have been through.

We hope that the Lord will see fit to bless us with more children to fill these empty arms.

We have accepted our misfortunes as being a part of life. Some folks think that we should go through a long mourning period and be bitter because others have children and we don't. But that attitude would solve nothing.

We three had such a happy time that only happy memories color our thinking.

I won't get a vacation this summer, but I think I can get several weeks in the fall. Probably in November. I think the weather would be nicer then, and the heat doesn't bother me.

It's strange that though we've met only once — some nine years ago this summer — I feel as close to all of you as though we were neighbors. Be assured that your letter helped us so very much.

Gratefully — Don

Many friends and family did their best to comfort Don and Ruth with kind words and gestures including Elizabeth Lewis who invited the grief-stricken couple to her family's home in Mesa, Arizona, to relax. They accepted her invitation but did not arrive until the fall. Don looked forward to the visit since he hadn't seen Elizabeth and her daughter Janet in almost ten years. He would be quite surprised to see Janet, now a young woman, greet them at the door.

Due to his general health and recent circumstances, Don moved into a new position as a machine operator at a clothing factory close to his home. He tried to find healthy distractions to avoid mulling, so he devoted much of his free time to the Boy Scouts. He also organized Firwood's first boys choir and assisted with the Sunday School classes.

Although Don and Ruth helped each other overcome the trauma caused by Ann's death, they worried they might never have another child because Ruth was 38 years old, which was considered too old to bare a child during that era. But even if she could have another child, they wondered if it too would be unhealthy.

Ruth and Don Byers pose for a picture with Jan and her father, Herman, at their home in Mesa.

1953

The new year seemed to prove to be a new start for the couple when they learned that Ruth was pregnant again. On October 19, she gave birth to a daughter, who they named after the girl who gave Don so much hope while he was at war and after Ann's death. Although preliminary tests showed no signs of major illnesses, it was later discovered that Janet was born with a hemangioma on her forehead. A hemangioma is a dense, elevated mass of dilated blood vessels. She was injected with medicines instead of resorting to surgery, and the condition was cured within a year.

February 24, 1955

Dear Lewises,

Takes a few days to finish a letter so I won't date this. Bad news first, my grandmother has had quite a time with bursitus. The pain was so bad that she had a nervous collapse. She'll be 87 next month. Ruth's uncle had an adrenal gland removed in an effort to bring his pressure down - that or go blind or out of his mind.

We take Jan for another check on the lump this Saturday. She had her first polio shot last week. Gets her second in three more weeks, then in seven months for the third.

I had my semi-annual check up by the doctor. My pressure is a little high but nothing to worry about. I believe in an "ounce of prevention".

We sure have been getting a lot of cold and snow this winter. Sure will be glad when spring and summer come along!

Ruth's having a time trying to potty train Jan. She's just too busy to tell us until after it's too late.

February 25

Ruth took Jan to the doctor today. He said the lump looks so good - smaller that is - that he won't want to see her for a year unless things get too bad. He'll wait indefinetly for the time to remove little scars, etc. He'll do it anytime we want, 1-5-10 years from now. So we feel very good about the news.

We hear from Big Jan from time to time. She seems to be having a fine time in school.

We all keep pretty well, except Ruth. She's tired and worn out all the time. She eats a lot but doesn't seem to gain any weight.

February 26

Just as we were getting Jan ready for Sunday School, she got sick. It's lasted all day, must be that 24-hour virus. We're kinda beat about now.

In the picture you'll see Jan's suitcase, dog, etc. For about three weeks she ironed everything in sight. Now she has other things on her mind.

Guess I better close this letter before January comes along!

Love to you and all the bees in the hive.

Ruth, Don, and Lil' Jan

Don was grateful for his second chance at fatherhood and spent as much time as possible with Janet. He occassionally took her along with him when he drove around town to do errands and to Boy Scout meetings. He expressed his jubilance in a letter to the Lewises:

"I'm eagerly awaiting for the time when Janet will be old enough to stand the long drive to Arizona to see her "western kin." With Jan so small we really can't go too far. I know that the Janets will have a wonderful time. At the rate she's going, Jan will be the only one who can keep up with her! Once she gets to walking and talking, we'll be too busy to think about growing old."

Almost ten years after the end of World War II, Don reminisced about the men he fought with in the valleys and mountains of Italy. He kept in contact with Pete Mason and other comrades, but wondered what had become of the others. He discussed organizing a reunion of the 337th during telephone conversations with fellow wiremen Don Lowe and Bill Mitchell. They decided to form a committee to assemble their fellow soldiers for a reunion in the summer of 1955. The three gathered about 17 men for the first reunion at the Mayflower Hotel in Akron, Ohio. They all enjoyed exchanging war stories and introducing their families to the men whom they had shared the most defining period of their lives. The men felt that the event was such a success that they decided to form a simple group to organize future gatherings. Byers served as treasurer for the 337th Infantry Regiment Reunion Organization and helped schedule a second reunion at the Ben Franklin Hotel in Philadelphia for the following year. The reunion's proximity to Don's old neighborhood allowed him the chance to visit friends and family he hadn't seen for some time.

The 337th reunions were the only times when Don spoke about his military service - even then he was tight lipped. He'd rather talk about the crap and card games then the fear and cynicism he sometimes felt. Although his experiences were not as grave as others, he witnessed death and the savagry of war. He never forgot the faces of the dead G.I.s he marched past and the proximity of bombs that exploded near him. He was grateful that he had survived World War II and was not about to brag or boast.

Reliving the past must have stirred something inside him because it was around this time that he began to document his years spent in the army. He wrote and typed his recollections about his state-side training, calling the story "My American Odyssey". As an avid reader, he likened his Workd War II experience to Homer's "The Odyssey", an ancient story about world travel and war. In between work, family, Masonic meetings, Boy Scout meetings, choir practice, and church masses Don spent time remembering and writing about being a soldier. His story was humorous and blunt, including every detail - and there was no reason to sugar coat anything.

As the new year began, the Byers were grappling with two family tragedies: Ruth's mother had passed away and Don's father began to suffer from a malignant melanoma on the right side of his face. Again, Don's chronic back pain interfered with his ability to work steadily, so he was forced to find yet another job - this time as a machine operator for Faith Shoe Company in Wilkes-Barre.

The upcoming fourth reunion of the 337th was a chance for Don to put his personal and physical problems aside for a while to enjoy the company of his old army buddies. Don was still the committee's treasurer and Pete Mason was in charge of the event which was held in the summer at the St. Charles Hotel in New Orleans.

As Don's eleventh wedding anniversary and forty-fourth birthday neared, his father was placed in a nursing home after he suf-

Ruth, Janet, and Don spending a summer afternoon together at Sylvan Lake, PA, in 1958.

fered a stroke and the cancerous growth on his face worsened. It was a difficult decision, but Adela was unable to tend to all of her husband's medical needs. Don made several weekend trips to visit, but he felt a bit guilty because he was unable to truly care for his parents. The fact was that he had his own family now and lived too far away to be of any real help.

On Friday, November 14, Don and his family traveled to Philadelphia to visit his mother at home and his father at the nursing home. On Sunday afternoon, Don felt ill so he called his old family doctor to the house. The doctor examined him and said he had a bad case of grip. Don felt too sick to drive the more than one hundred miles back to Wilkes-Barre so he climbed into the backseat of the car with a pillow and blanket while Ruth drove with Janet at her side. As soon as they arrived home, he went right into the house and into bed.

On Tuesday, Don collapsed when he tried to walk to the bathroom. Ruth had to ask some neighbors to help get him back into bed. She spent the next few days tending to her husband, who now had a 103 degree temperature. By Thursday, his fever broke but he felt paralyzed and had difficulty breathing so Ruth called the family doctor. Don was given a shot of penicillin, and the doctor suggested that if his condition worsened that he be admitted to the General Hospital. The next day, the doctor returned to see Don when his breathing became labored and decided to admit him to the hospital. The staff tried to accommodate their patient, but they soon realized that they could not adequately treat him, so he was transferred to the Veterans Hospital.

When they arrived at the Veterans Hospital, the doctor asked Ruth to sign a consent form that permitted him to perform a tracheotomy on Don. After the operation, the doctor escorted Ruth into his office for a cup of coffee and to discuss her husband's health. The doctor believed that his condition wouldn't drastically change overnight so he advised her to go home.

As soon as she got home, the doctor called to tell her that Don's condition had taken a turn for the worst. Ruth raced back to the hospital, but she learned that her husband had died only a few moments before she arrived. The doctor couldn't immediately diag-

nose the cause of his death, so he requested an autopsy.

The attending doctor's report states the final days of Don's life:

"On the weekend of November 15, 1958, the couple visited Philadelphia. The patient seemed somewhat "grippy". Following his return home from Philadelphia, he continued to feel somewhat ill, and on Monday morning he had a temperature of 103.5. His family doctor was consulted, who told his wife the patient had an attack of virus infection and he was given penicillin. On November 18, his temperature subsided, but that night he complained that his legs were paralyzed. On the 19th, he complained of shortness of breath and inability to void. The doctor came and catheterized him. On November 20, he was completely paralyzed. He could not move his arms or legs and on the evening of the 21st he had difficulty in talking and swallowing. The doctor again visited him, and at 1 p.m. he was taken to the Wilkes-Barre General Hospital, placed in oxygen, was given intravenous solutions, catheterized, and x-rays were taken.

Patient was transferred from the General Hospital to the VA Hospital at 9:30 p.m. as an emergency because of a flaccid paralysis of all extremities, respiratory failure, and no availability of facilities for treatment of what they suspected to be poliomyelitis. The patient was brought to the admission office, where an emergency tracheotomy was done because of marked cyanosis, respiratory failure, and paralysis of the pharynx. Following the tracheotomy, he received emergency treatment and respiratory stimulants were given. The patient's blood pres-

sure gradually dropped and in spite of all
efforts. The patient expired at 1:50 a.m."

The funeral and burial for Don was well attended by the friends
he had made in Wilkes-Barre and a few who traveled from Philadelphia. His Uncle Harry and cousin Nancy escorted his mother Adela,
but his father George couldn't attend due to his progressed cancer.
(George died weeks later in December.) Members from the Caldwell
Consistory conducted a Masonic Funeral, Boy Scout Troop 55 pre-
sented a memorial placque to the family, and Military Funeral
Honors were held. Don was buried at Oak Lawn Cemetery near
Ann. The autopsy results weren't completed by the time of his funeral, but the coroner's results later revealed that Don had indeed contracted poliomyelitis (polio).

Polio was a common, contagious, epidemic viral infection,
which is usually confined to children, but can also affect adults.
Polio is an inflammation of the brain and spinal cord caused by a
virus that enters the body through the nose or mouth and is carried
by the bloodstream to the central nervous system where it enters a
nerve cell. The virus multiplies so rapidly that it quickly damages or
kills the cell. Paralysis results when many cells are destroyed, but
that doesn't always leave the victim paralyzed. In fact, infection by
a polio virus doesn't always result in severe illness. Some persons
exhibit simple symptoms such as fever, headache, sore throat, or
vomiting that might only last for twenty-four hours then disappear.
These symptoms are common in many ailments and might lead to
misdiagnosis.

Since polio is a disease more commonly suffered by children,
Don and his doctor did not consider it as the real reason for his sud-
den illness. Plus his pre-existing back condition seems to have
masked the symptoms of polio which can be confused with the flu
and other viruses - so misdiagnosis is possible. And by the time he
received medical attention, the disease had incubated and was full
blown. Even if he had received the vaccine, it probably would have
had no positive effects to save his life. What is more puzzling is how
he contracted the disease: was it from a patient at his father's nursing home or a child in the choir or Boy Scout troop?

Ruth and Janet stayed with family for a few days after Don's death. She was overwhelmed with emotions considering that she had lost a daughter, mother, and husband within the past six years. But she realized that they had to return home and carry on with their lives. Ruth focused on caring for Janet the best that she could as a single mother. She had her job at the bank as well as income from tenants who rented apartments in her double-block home. They received help from family when it was necessary, but being someone who had lived through the Great Depression, Ruth had a strong sense of pride and knew how to stretch a dollar.

Each night, Ruth and Janet sat on their front porch together to relax. She would point to a bright star and tell the little girl that the glimmering light was her father looking down from heaven. Janet would stare at the tiny sparkle of light trying to make sense of it, wondering where her daddy went and why he left.

Bibliography:

While writing this book, the Editor referred to the following books, publications, and websites to confirm information.

Books and Publications:
* 5th Army Group, *Road to Rome*. Italy. 1945.
* 3196th Signal Service Company, *A History of the 3196th Signal Service Company*. Leghorn. August 1945.
* Schultz, Paul, L. T*he 85th Infantry Division in World War II*. Infantry Journal Press.
  Washington. 1949.
* Starr, Chester G. *Fifth Army History*. L'Impronta Press. Florence, Italy. 1945.
* Paul, John R. *History of Poliomyelitis*. Connecticut Printers, Inc. Hartford, Conn. 1971.
* Dougherty, Robert A. and Gruber, Ira D., *World War II: Total Warfare Around the Globe*. D.C. Heath and Co., Lexington, Mass. 1996.
* *85th Infantry Division, Minturno to Appennines*. 85th Infantry Division. 1945.
* *Rome-Arno*. U.S. Government Press Office, Washington D.C. 1994.
* *Anzio*. U.S. Government Press Office, Washington D.C. 1994.
* *The Stars and Stripes, Mediterranean*. Volume 1, Number 154, May 19, 1944.
* *The Stars and Stripes, Mediterranean*. Volume 1, Number 229, April 13, 1945.
* *Custer Combateer*, Volume 1, Number 3, May 19, 1945.
* *Wolverine Weekly*, Volume 1, Number 7, June 30, 1945.
* *The Wilkes-Barre Record*, (The Times Leader), Nov. 24, 1958.
* *The Philadelphia Inquirer*, Nov. 24, 1958.
* A variation of **My American Odyssey** previously appeared in *manifest magazine*, August 2005, Byers Publishing, Inc.

Websites:
* www.337thinfantry.net
* www.army.mil
* www.milhist.net
* www.custermen.com

Other:
* 337th Regimental Monthly Report, January 1944 - August 1945.
* 85th Division Monthly Report, May 1945 - August 1945.

Acknowledgements:

It is unknown what other short stories, notes, or letters existed about Don Byers' military and personal life. Many of his photographs and keepsakes were destroyed when a flood caused by Tropical Storm Agnes washed out his widow's home in Wilkes-Barre, in 1972. A year later, a fire destroyed thousands of military records kept at the National Personnel Records Center in St. Louis. Those events caused the Editor to conduct more research than is usually necessary for people to obtain information about veterans' military service.

The following people provided or helped the Editor collect information that aided the research, writing, and printing of this book:

* *Bill & Marjorie Mitchell, 337th Infantry Regiment Reunion Organization*
* *Donald Lowe, 337th Infantry*
* *Hubert Speck, 337th Infantry*
* *Don Jones, 337thinfantry.net*
* *National Archives at College Park, Md.*
* *Pennsylvania Department of Health*
* *Department of Veterans Affairs*
* *Temple University, Philadelphia, Pa.*
* *Social Security Administration*
* *Free Library of Philadelphia*
* *Philadelphia's Vital Records Department*
* *Janet (Lewis) Miller*
* *Ruth Byers*
* *Janet Ruth Byers*
* *Adela Byers*
* *Michael Donald Hivish*
* *Cassandra Adela Hivish*
* *David Evans, OPM, Dallas, PA*
* *Andrew Petonak, Luzerne Co. Community College, Nanticoke, PA*
* *Dr. Walter Brasch, Bloomsburg University, Bloomsburg, Pa.*
* *Former Congressman Paul Kanjorski (PA-11)*

About the Editor

James Byers was born in Wilkes-Barre, in 1975. He graduated from Bloomsburg University with a bachelors degree in communications. He later earned an associates degree in Political Science from Luzerne County Community College.

Throughout his career, he has worked in the print industry as a newspaper reporter, publishing assistant, and a graphic artist. He founded **Byers Publishing** *in 2005. In 2010, Jim became a Master Mason and wears the same Masonic ring worn by his grandfather.*

Made in the USA
Lexington, KY
20 May 2017